Sign Language Fun
in the
Early Childhood Classroom

Enrich Language and Literacy Skills of Young Hearing Children, Children with Special Needs, and English Language Learners

by
Sherrill B. Flora

illustrated by
Chris Olsen

My name (is) _____.

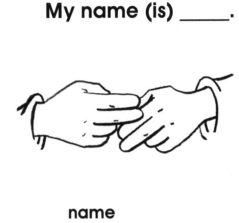

My

Place the palm of the right hand flat on the chest.

name

Both hands make the letter "U" and then cross each other to form an "X."

Fingerspell your name.

What (is) your name?

What

The right pointer finger passes over the palm of the left hand.

your

The flat right hand, palm facing out and fingers together, moves forward.

name

Both hands make the letter "U" and then cross each other to form an "X."

Key Education
An imprint of Carson-Dellosa Publishing, LLC
Greensboro, North Carolina

keyeducationpublishing.com

CONGRATULATIONS ON YOUR PURCHASE OF A KEY EDUCATION PRODUCT!

The editors at Key Education are former teachers who bring experience, enthusiasm, and quality to each and every product. Thousands of teachers have looked to the staff at Key Education for new and innovative resources to make their work more enjoyable and rewarding. Key Education is committed to developing and publishing educational materials that will assist teachers in building a strong and developmentally appropriate curriculum for young children.

PLAN FOR GREAT TEACHING EXPERIENCES WHEN YOU USE
EDUCATIONAL MATERIALS FROM KEY EDUCATION PUBLISHING

References

Acredolo, L., Goodwyn, S. (1996). *Baby signs: how to talk with your baby before your baby can talk.* Contemporary: Chicago. 5–7.

Capirci, O., Cattani, A., Rossinni P., Volterra, V. (1998). "Teaching sign language to hearing children as a possible factor in cognitive enhancement." Journal of Deaf Studies and Deaf Education 3:2 Spring, 135–142.

Daniels, M. (1993). "ASL as a possible factor in the acquisition of English for hearing children." Sign Language Studies, 78, 25–30.

Daniels, M. (2001). *Dancing with words: signing for hearing children's literacy.* Westport, Connecticut: Bergin and Garvey.

Daniels, M. (1994). "The effects of sign language on hearing children's language development." Sign Language Studies, 78, 25–30.

Emunds, M., Krupinski, D. (2006). "Using sign language and fingerspelling to facilitate early literacy skills." From the Start: A Ready to Learn Resource for PreK-2 Educators. PBS.

Felzer, L. (2000). "Research on how signing helps hearing children learn to read." MBR Beginning Reading Program, California State University, Pomona.

Wills, K. (1981). "Manual communication training for non-speaking hearing children." Journal of Pediatric Psychology (1) 15–27.

Credits

Author: Sherrill B.Flora
Creative Director: Annette Hollister-Papp
Inside Illustrations: Chris Olsen
Editors: George C. Flora and
      Karen Seberg
Production: Key Education Staff

FINGER NAMES AND HAND POSITIONS

The following chart illustrates the finger names and hand positions used in the sign descriptions featured in this book:

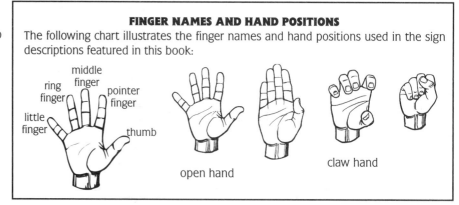

open hand   claw hand

Key Education

An imprint of Carson-Dellosa Publishing, LLC
PO Box 35665
Greensboro, NC 27425 USA
keyeducationpublishing.com

Printed in the USA · All rights reserved.

ISBN 978-1-933052-49-6
02-364138091

Contents

Introduction:
An Important Message

Sign Language Fun in the Early Childhood Classroom is an educational resource designed for **ALL** early childhood classrooms and is to be used by **ALL** teachers, care providers, and parents of **ALL** young children: hearing, hearing-impaired, deaf, children with special needs, gifted children, children with communication disorders, and children who are new to our country and are just learning to speak English (ELL). Teachers and parents **DO NOT** need any previous knowledge or experience with American Sign Language (ASL) to successfully use this book.

Sign Language Fun in the Early Childhood Classroom provides you with:

1. Information (based on research) about why American Sign Language is an effective early childhood teaching strategy that can:
    - accelerate verbal communication;
    - increase English vocabulary, attentional abilities, visual discrimination, and spatial memory; and,
    - can enhance early reading skills, such as comprehension, sight word recognition, phonemic awareness, phonetic and spelling skills.

2. Easy-to-use thematic teaching units, complete with teaching suggestions, games, activities, songs, rhymes, recommended children's literature, and reproducible illustrated sign language cards to get you started **learning** and **teaching** ASL to your eager young learners!

What We Have Learned from Research!

The Deaf Community: American Sign Language (ASL) is the third most widely used language in the United States and is an official "foreign language" that is being taught at many high schools. The history of "sign language" includes the first manual alphabet, written by Juan Pablo de Bonet in 1620; in 1755 Abbé Charles-Michel de l'Épée began the first public education for the deaf in France; and in 1816 Thomas Hopkins Gallaudet convinced the Frenchman Laurent Clerc to travel from France to become the first deaf sign-language teacher in America. In short, sign language has been a highly-effective communication system in America for almost 200 years, and was developed by deaf people to enable the deaf community to communicate with each other. However, ASL was not considered to be a true language until 1960 when William Stokoe published his book titled *Sign Language Structure*.

A Proven Communication System for Hearing Students with Special Needs: Educators believed (*and have found to be true*) that sign language can increase the communication skills of hearing children with particular pathologies such as Downs Syndrome, various forms of developmental delays, and more recently autism and other forms of communication disorders. In 1981, in a research study where sign language was taught to nonverbal children (Wills, 1981), it showed that 92% of those children acquired some communication skills. It was also shown that when both the teachers and parents used the signs that the children learned during their signing lessons, that the children were more likely to generalize the use of those signs in other settings. Following the success of the deaf community, children with special needs were the next group to have garnered the benefits from learning sign language.

An Early Communication System for Infants: For the past few years the new "buzz" has been that infants can learn to "talk through sign language" before actually learning to "talk!" Between the ages of 9 and 30 months a baby's desire to talk usually exceeds his ability to speak. Recent research has documented (Acredolo, 1996) that not only can infants learn to sign (*use gestural symbols*) to express words, but that infants who are taught to sign can demonstrate an increased process of learning to speak, and that it provides intellectual stimulation, and more importantly, it has been shown to strengthen the bond between parent and baby.

An Accelerated Communication Strategy for Children Who Are Learning English: Some of the latest research has focused on understanding the effect that learning sign language has on the developing language skills of English language learners. The first studies were conducted almost accidently. It was observed that hearing children of deaf parents were able to acquire sign language and spoken language at the same time. These children often showed rapid language development and very quickly became bilingual. In another study (Daniels, 1993), it was shown that bilingual children receiving sign language instruction scored higher on the Peabody Picture Vocabulary Test (PPVT) than their peers who did not receive any signing instruction. This provides evidence that ASL has a positive effect on young children's acquisition of English.

The Effect of ASL on Increasing the Language and Literacy Skills of Young Hearing Children: The most exciting research currently being conducted is focused on documenting the effects that learning sign language has on the development of language and literacy skills of young hearing children. In two different studies (Capirci, 1998) ASL was taught in context to children during their first and second grade years. The children in both studies who received the instruction scored higher on tests in visual discrimination and spatial memory than did the groups of children who did not receive any signing instruction. Additional studies (Daniels, 1994) have consistently found that young hearing children of hearing parents who learned ASL in a school context, demonstrated a greater understanding of English vocabulary and achieved higher scores on the PPVT than their peers who did not receive any instruction.

It has also been documented that when young children are ready to learn how to read, that the learning of sign language can strengthen and increase oral language and literacy skills. It was observed that hearing children of deaf parents were often reading before they began school because their parents had fingerspelled with them. The researchers concluded that these children were able to make the connection between the manual letters of fingerspelling and the printed letters on a page. We have also learned a great deal about multiple intelligences from Howard Gardner– and the importance of understanding and identifying the wide variety of individual learning styles as well as the importance of multi-sensory teaching. Sign language involves seeing, hearing, and movement. This is the perfect combination of how young children learn best. Using the multi-sensory approaches of sign language, children are able to use both sides of the brain, thus creating multiple pathways which can strengthen memory and build connections for further learning.

In Conclusion, teaching sign language has incredible benefits for all young children. Its multi-sensory approach increases and builds language and literacy skills, motivates young learners through their natural desire for constant movement, and provides an atmosphere of play and fun! Sounds like the perfect learning tool!

Getting Started

Getting Started—The Most Important Rule: "Know the signs before you teach them!" Review each chapter and learn the signs before you begin to teach. You should feel comfortable with the signs by the time you introduce them to the children. Write lesson plans and determine "how much" and "how quickly" your children will be able to absorb.

What to Do with the Reproducible Illustrated Sign Language Cards: There is a reproducible illustrated sign language card for each sign taught in this book. These cards are found at the end of each chapter. They are an important tool for learning all of the signs. Before beginning to teach a chapter make sure you that have made two copies of each illustrated sign language card for every child in your class. You should also make a copy of each card for the Classroom Sign Word Wall.

1. **Classroom Sign Word Wall:** Each time a new sign is introduced add it to the Classroom Word Wall. The children can use the word wall as a reference to review signs, and the cards can be used for memory games and activities. The children will also enjoy watching the wall fill-up with words. They will be able to "see" how much they are learning.

2. **My Own Sign Language Dictionary:** Give all of the children an illustrated sign language card each time a new sign is introduced. Each child can color the picture on the card and tape or glue it onto a page in their "My Own Sign Language Dictionary." During quiet times or free time the children can look through their own books and practice the signs.

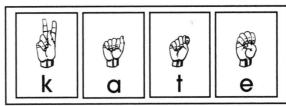
listen
The hand is cupped behind the ear –
implying that the ears should listen.

3. **Send a Copy of Each Illustrated Sign Language Card Home to the Parents:** Sending home these cards will encourage parents to take an active interest in what their children are learning at school. Tell the parents that they should ask their children to teach the family the new signs that they have learned at school. The parents should also try to use the signs at home so that learning is reinforced at both home and school.

The Importance of Fingerspelling: Please read "What We Have Learned from Research" on page 4. It provides evidence of the importance of teaching children how to fingerspell the alphabet. This should be taught when the children are ready to learn alphabet letters–usually by kindergarten. Reproducible illustrated fingerspelling alphabet cards have been included on pages 6–8. When you are teaching the letters of the alphabet, introduce the signs for those letters at the same time.

1. **Teach the Children to Fingerspell Their Own Names:** Provide the children with a copy of the fingerspelling letter cards for their own names. Cut them out and tape or glue them to a piece of card stock. Send it home and have the children practice learning how to fingerspell their own names.

2. **Introduce a Signed Letter Each Time a Print Letter Is Introduced:** Give the children an illustrated sign language letter card (pages 6–8) each time a new letter is introduced. Copy the letter and have the children add it to their "My Own Sign Language Dictionary."

k	a	t	e

Lesson one: Sign Hello/Good-bye: This is the best sign to use when introducing the concept of sign language. Discuss what it might be like to be deaf and then explain sign language to the children. How many children have heard about sign language? Tell them that they will be learning to talk with their hands.

Ask them what they think would be a good sign for the words "hello" and "good-bye." There is a high probability the children will sign a "wave of the hands." Talk about how many of the signs they will be learning will make sense to them. The signs often help visualize the word. Copy the "hello/good-bye" card and make this the first card on the classroom word wall and in the children's sign language dictionaries.

hello/good-bye
The open hand waves back and forth.
It means both hello and good-bye.

a

b

c

d

e

f

g

h

i

j

k

l

m

n

o

p

q

r

s

t

u

v

w

x

y

z

-8-

Sign Language Fun in the Early Childhood Classroom

Chapter One

Manners and Words Used Throughout the Day

> **13 Signs to Be Learned:** cleanup, good, listen, no, please, share, sing, sorry, thank-you, toilet, wash, watch, yes
>
> *(Reproduce the illustrated sign language cards found on pages 10–12. Make a copy for each child's "My Own Sign Language Dictionary," the Classroom Sign Word Wall, and one to be sent home to each child's parents.)*

Getting Started: Young children learn signs faster if they are first taught signs that are meaningful to them and represent either words, personal needs, or actions that occur commonly throughout the children's day. This gives the children an opportunity to use the signs frequently and to observe the signs being used.

Introduce the above signs following the order of the activities below. Most of the signs are introduced through games and activities which allows the children to use the signs in context while having fun practicing their new language skills.

Teach the Signs for Yes and No: The children should have already learned the sign for "hello" and "good-bye." This sign should have made sense to the children because it is just like waving "hello" or "good-bye." The sign for the word "yes" will also make sense to the children. The fist forms the letter "s" and then nods up and down, just like a head nodding "yes." "No" is not as obvious. The index and middle fingers tap the thumb similar to the movement of a bird's beak opening and closing. A great way to learn these signs is through the song, "Who Stole the Cookie from the Cookie Jar?" and for answering silly questions that require a "yes" or "no" answer.

Who Took the Cookies from the Cookie Jar?

Who took the cookies from the cookie jar?
(*Child's name*) took the cookies from the cookie jar.

Who me?	*(Solo sung by the child whose name was chosen.)*
Yes, you!	*(All children sign "yes.")*
No, not me!	*(Child signs "no.")*
Then who?	

(*Another child's name*) took the cookies from the cookie jar.

Who me?	*(Solo sung by the child whose name was chosen.)*
Yes, you!	*(All children sign "yes.")*
No, not me!	*(Child signs "no.")*
Then who?	

Silly Questions:

Have the children sign either "yes" or "no" when the teacher asks some silly questions, such as the following:

1. Are you a kangaroo?
2. Do you want to eat some mud?
3. Do you live in a submarine?

Also ask questions that allow them to use the "yes" sign.

Teach the Signs for Toilet and Wash: To sign the word " toilet," the hand forms the letter "t" and is then shaken. This is a fun sign for the children to use when asking to go to the restroom – a sign that most definitely will be used several times each day. Also teach the children how to sign the word "wash." Use this opportunity to discuss with the children when they should wash their hands and the proper way to wash hands. Set up several wash basins and fill them with warm water and bubbles. Let the children practice signing their new vocabulary while having fun playing with the bubbles.

When to Wash: · Before eating or making something to eat · After playing outside · After playing with pets · After using the bathroom · After blowing their noses, coughing, or sneezing. · When hands look dirty. **How to Wash:** · Wash for 20 seconds using warm running water and liquid soap · Scrub palms, backs, between fingers, under fingernails, wrists and thumbs · Turn off the faucet with a paper towel to avoid recontamination · Thoroughly dry hands, preferably with a paper towel

The Magic Words are Please, Thank-You, and Sorry: These words should be used frequently throughout the day. Learn the signs by following the directions on the illustrated sign language cards (pages 11–12). Use the following activities to help the children practice using the signs for the magic words.

The Magic Words Bulletin Board: Have each child make a "magic wand" and label the wands with the children's names. (*See illustration.*) Each time you see a child using one of the magic word signs, place a gold sticker on that child's wand. The children will love watching their magic wands fill up with stars!

The Magic Words Tea Party: Let the children have a pretend tea party during snack time. Use tea cups filled with hot chocolate or apple cider and a plate of cookies or crackers while encouraging them to practice using the magic word signs.

Catch 'em Being GOOD: This is a sign that the teacher should use often. The more often a teacher tells children that they are being "good," the more likely that children will want to be "good!" Encourage the children to use the "good" sign when they are playing with their friends. Make it a classroom challenge that everyone should try to catch each other being "good!"

Teacher Directions—Watch, Listen, Sing, and Share: The words "watch, listen, sing, and share" are common words used by early childhood teachers. The teacher should introduce these words to the children by first showing the children each sign and then having them guess what each sign could mean.

The children will probably guess the correct meaning for the signs "listen" and "watch." They may also guess the sign for "sing" because it looks as if one is conducting a choir.

Finally, the sign for "share" is a wonderful reminder sign for the children. Sharing is not always easy during the early childhood years. The children will probably not be able to guess the meaning of this sign at first, but once it is explained to them that the sign actually represents something being divided into two parts – dividing something to be shared, it should be more easily remembered. Use these signs often throughout the day and you may begin to see the children attempting to use them properly as well.

Cleanup Fun: This is a sign that is needed throughout the day in every early childhood classroom. Teach the children the sign for "cleanup" and then teach them "The Classroom Cleanup Song." Each time the children hear the word "cleanup," they should also do the "cleanup" sign. As the children become more comfortable, they should sing the song, but not sing the words "cleanup." They should just use the sign for "cleanup."

The Cleanup Song
(*Sung to "A Hunting We Will Go"*)
It's time to cleanup our room.
It's time to cleanup our room.
We all say "yes" to pick up our mess
It's fun to cleanup our room!

cleanup
With the hands flat,
one hand wipes off the other hand.

good

The flat hand moves from touching the mouth to being in front of the body, as if something was tasted.

listen

The hand is cupped behind the ear – implying that the ears should listen.

no

The pointer finger and the middle finger together tap the thumb, similar to a bird's beek opening and closing.

please

The hand is open and flat and moves in a circular motion on the chest.

share

Both hands are opened with the fingers together. The movement of the hands represent dividing up things that are to be shared.

sing

The right hand is open and waves back and forth above the left arm, as if conducting a choir.

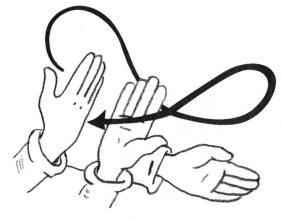

sorry

The fist moves in a circular motion over the heart.

thank-you

The hand, with all four fingers touching the lips, moves forward a few inches.

toilet

Make the letter "T" and then shake the fist.

wash

The right hand makes the letter "A" and moves in a circular (washing) motion over the other hand that is also making the letter "A."

watch

The hand makes the letter "V," palm side of the hand toward the body. The hand touches the eyes and then swings back out so the fingers are pointing forward.

yes

The hand makes the letter "S" and then moves up and down like a head nodding.

Following Directions/Movement

> **10 Signs to Be Learned:** come, dance, go, jump, roll, run, sit, stand, stop, walk
>
> *(Reproduce the illustrated sign language cards found on pages 15–16. Make a copy for each child's "My Own Sign Language Dictionary," the Classroom Sign Word Wall, and one to be sent home to each child's parents.)*

Getting Started: In Chapter One the children learned 13 signs that they will be able to use throughout the day that encourage nice manners, good behavior, and positive attitudes. The signs taught in Chapter Two take advantage of one of the most effective ways that young children learn – through movement.

During the early childhood years children often learn best by "doing." Movement and multi-sensory experiences are essential for all young children, but are even more important for children who learn best through "kinesthetic" approaches. This chapter provides the essential "learn by doing" technique that incorporates a child's natural love of movement, motion, and activity. Not only are the signs taught in this chapter a great deal of fun for the children to learn, but they also help young children increase their listening skills and their ability to follow directions.

In this chapter the signs "come, go and stop" are taught first, then the sign for "dance," and finally the six remaining movement signs: "jump, roll, run, sit, stand, and walk." The six movement signs can be taught in any order and can be used with any of the following movement games and activities.

Teach the Signs Come, Go, and Stop: These three signs each reflect the meaning of its word. "Come" is a beckoning "come here" gesture; the sign for "go" has the fingers pointing away and looking as if you are telling a person to "go" away; and the sign for "stop" looks like a gate coming down that would "stop" someone from moving any further. Once again, demonstrate each sign for the children and then have them guess the meaning of each sign. Make a list of the guesses and then make a graph of the responses. Which idea has the most? The least? How many children guessed the correct meaning of each sign?

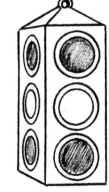

Come, Go, and Stop Red Light/Green Light: Play this version of Red Light/Green Light with the children. You will need either a large room, gymnasium, or playground. Have the children stand in a line. When the teacher signs "come," the children should begin to walk forward. When the teacher signs "stop," the children should stop. Finally, when the teacher signs "go," the children should walk backwards. *(Come– walk forward; stop– everyone stops; go– walk backwards.)* Have the children first practice by simultaneously using both signs and words. After the children are familiar with the directions, play the game only with signs. If a sign is misunderstood, the child takes two giant steps backward. If a sign is understood, the child takes two giant steps forward. The first children over the finish line are the winners!

Teach the Sign for Dance: All young children seem to love to dance! The combination of music and movement always makes for a favorite activity. The sign for "dance" is a lot of fun. The fingers actually look as if they are dancing. Have the children practice the sign for "dance" while singing and signing the song below:

Dance around the Circle
(Sung to the tune of "Ring around the Rosie")
Dance around the circle.
Dance around the circle.
We dance. We dance. We love to dance!

More Dancing: This is an activity that will delight the children. The teacher should prepare small construction paper dancers, approximately three to four inches tall. The teacher can either draw their own dancers, or cut out pictures of people dancing from magazines or coloring books. Glue a large paper clip on the back of each dancer. Hold the dancer on a piece of cardboard or on a cookie sheet. Place a magnet behind the board or cookie sheet and then move the magnet to make the dancer "dance." The children will have lots of fun with this activity. One child can manipulate the dancer while the other children can sing and sign the song "Dance around the Circle" (see page 13).

Dancing with Streamers: Give the children scarfs and/or streamers. Ask one child to be the signer. When the child signs the word "dance," have all the children dance and swing their streamers. When the signer signs "stop," the children should stop dancing.

The following games and activities use these Chapter Two movement signs: dance, jump, roll, run, sit, stand, and walk.

Teach the Signs for Dance, Jump, Roll, Run, Sit, Stand, and Walk: Demonstrate the signs and have the children brainstorm a list of what they think each sign means.

Stand, walk, and Sit "Silent" Musical Chairs: The teacher places chairs back-to-back in two lines. There should be one less chair than there are children playing. Instead of listening to music, the children will follow the teacher's signing instructions: "stand, walk, and sit." When the teacher signs "walk," have the children walk around the chairs. As soon as the teacher signs "sit," the children should find a chair and sit as quickly as possible. The child without a chair is the next person to sign the instructions. Remove another chair and have the child sign "stand." All the children stand and are ready to begin again.

Monkey See/Monkey Do: This game is similar to "Follow the Leader." One child is chosen to be the "leader" of the monkeys. The "leader" of the monkeys will make the signs, one at a time: "dance, jump, roll, run, sit, stand, or walk." The rest of the monkeys (*all the other children*) will perform the action that is being signed by the "leader" of the monkeys. If a child performs a wrong movement that child must sit down. The last child standing is the winner and the next "leader" of the monkeys.

Obstacle Course: Set up an obstacle course using cones, boxes, mats, hoola-hoops, or whatever else you may have available. Tell the children that they will go through the obstacle course one at a time. The children can jump, roll, run, or walk on the obstacle course. As the one child is performing the actions the other children should make the correct sign for that action.

Jumping, Rolling, Running, or Walking Races: The children should each find a partner– one child will be partner A and one child will be partner B. All of the partner A's stand at the back of the room and all of the partner B's stand at the other end of the room. The teacher signs the movements for the partner A's first. Partner A's will have to jump, roll, run, or walk to the partner B side of the room. Once each partner A is close to their partner B, the partners should "tag" each other by clapping hands. The partner B's will then follow the teacher's movement signs to get to the other side of the room.

Song—Jump, Jump (*Sung to the Tune "Skip to My Lou"*): Use the signs for "dance, jump, roll, run, sit, stand, and walk" in the blanks. Do not say or sing the action words. Act out the song as it is being signed and sung. _____, _____, _____ to my Lou.   _____, _____, _____ to my Lou.
_____, _____, _____ to my Lou.   _____ to my Lou my darling.

Shadow Fun: First put up a movie screen, or hang a sheet over a chart stand or on a shower curtain rod placed in a doorway. Then create a light source using either a lamp, a large flashlight, or an overhead projector several feet behind the screen. One child at a time will get to perform behind the screen. The teacher secretly shows the child a movement sign: "dance, jump, roll, run, sit, stand, or walk." The child then goes behind the screen and performs the action. The other children watch the "shadow" child and then sign the action that they thought the shadow child was performing. How many children were able to make the correct sign?

(Illustrated Sign Language Cards)

Simon Says: This game is played exactly like "Simon Says," except it only uses sign language. At first the teacher should be Simon. Instead of saying "Simon Says," the teacher will sign "please" and then a "movement sign," such as "Please sit," "Please stand," "Please roll," or "Please jump." The children can only move if the word "please" is signed before the movement sign. If the teacher just signs "sit" or "stand," and does not include the sign for "please," the children should NOT move.

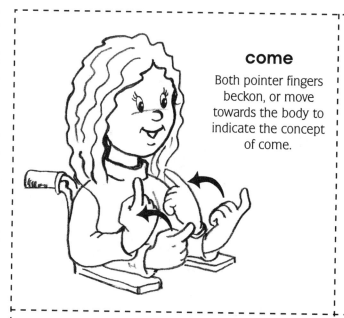

come

Both pointer fingers beckon, or move towards the body to indicate the concept of come.

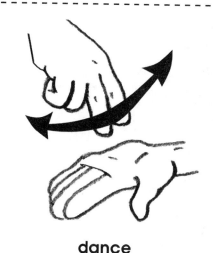

dance

The right hand is held in an upside down "V" and then dances on the palm of the left hand.

go

Both pointer fingers move in an arch and point away from the body.

jump

The right hand is held in an upside down "V" position and jumps up and down on the palm of the left hand.

roll

Both hands, with the pointer fingers extended, roll over each other without touching.

run

Each hand looks like a slightly bent letter "L." The pointer finger of one hand pulls on the thumb of the other hand as both hands move forward.

While the hands move forward the extended thumb and pointer finger are wiggled.

sit

The right pointer and middle fingers are draped over the same two fingers on the left hand. The fingers look like they are sitting.

stand

The right hand is held in an upside down "V" and stands on the palm of the left hand.

stop

With both hands open, the right hand with the little finger down strikes the left hand palm.

walk

With both hands flat, fingers pointing forward and held in front of the chest, the hands sway back and forth as if they are walking.

Chapter Three

Feelings/Emotions

> **10 Signs to Be Learned:** funny, happy, How do you feel?, I love you, mad, sad, scared, sick, tired, What's wrong?
>
> *(Reproduce the illustrated sign language cards found on pages 19–20. Make a copy for each child's "My Own Sign Language Dictionary," the Classroom Sign Word Wall, and one to be sent home to each child's parents.)*

Getting Started: Feelings/emotions is a theme that most early childhood programs explore with young children. Children need to learn how to identify these emotions in themselves and in others. Many of the ASL signs for feelings and emotions are fun for the children to make because when the hand gestures are combined with a facial expression, it can make the meaning of the sign much more powerful.

Before introducing any of this chapter's signs, **brainstorm a list** of feelings and emotions with the children. Write the list on a black board, a wipe off board, or on chart paper. After each emotion, ask for a volunteer to come up and draw a picture of that emotion.

Have a Mirror Available: Have the children take turns making "emotional" faces in the mirror. Ask them what they think they look like when they are sad. What do they think they look like when they are happy? What do they think they look like when they are scared? An understanding of each emotion will help the children to learn the signs for emotions much faster.

Teach the Signs Funny, Happy, Mad, Sad, Scared, Sick, and Tired: Introduce these signs to the children. They are fun to practice and are fairly easy to remember. To help the children learn these signs sing the song, "If You're Happy and You Know It" and have the children substitute different emotion signs (*funny, happy, mad, sad, scared, sick, tired*) in the blanks while singing the song.

If You're Happy and You Know It

If you're _____ and you know it, clap your hands.
If you're _____ and you know it, clap your hands.
If you're _____ and you know it, then your face will really show it.
If you're _____ and you know it, clap your hands.

How Do You Feel? Bulletin Board: Create a bulletin board with labels of happy, sad, mad, and scared. Use the illustrated sign language cards on pages 19–20 for this activity. Copy and enlarge the signs and place them on the bulletin board. Then take a photograph of each child and print each child's name on the bottom of the photo. Have the children pin their pictures under the sign for how they feel.

Pretend You Are a Mirror: Each child should have a partner. The partners sit facing each other. One child signs an emotion and the other child should then make a face that represents that emotion.

Memory Matching: Copy two sets of the feelings and emotions illustrated sign language cards found on pages 19–20 onto card stock. Color, cut-out, and laminate for durability. Use these cards to play memory matching. Each time a child picks up a pair of cards he should make the sign on the cards. If the cards match, the child may keep them. If the cards do not match, they are turned back over and the play passes to the next child.

Feeling and Emotion Literature: Read any good children's book about feelings and emotions. Each time an emotions word is used in the text have the children make the correct sign. Not only will the children enjoy some wonderful books, but it will help them remember the signs for feelings and emotions.

Children's Literature Featuring Specific Feelings:

- *The Boy Who Didn't Want to Be Sad* by Rob Goldblatt (Magination Press ©2004)
- *I Love You As Much . . .* by Laura Krauss Melmed (HarperTrophy; Reprint edition ©2005)
- *I Was So Mad* by Mercer Mayer (Golden Books ©2000)
- *Mother, Mother, I Feel Sick; Send for the Doctor, Quick, Quick, Quick* by Remy Charlip and Burton Supree (Tricycle Press ©2001)
- *Mr. Funny (Mr. Men and Little Miss)* by Roger Hargreaves (Stern Sloan ©1997)
- *Ten Tired Teddies Storytime Bed* by Prue Theobalds (John Hunt Publishing Limited ©2000)
- *What's Wrong and Other Mixed Up Fun* by Inc. Highlights for Children (Highlights for Children ©1990)
- *When I Feel Scared* by Cornelia Maude Spelman (Albert Whitman & Company; Reprint edition ©2004)
- *When You Are Happy* by Eileen Spinelli (Simon & Schuster Children's Publishing ©2006)

Children's Literature Featuring More Than One Feeling:

- *Do Animals Have Feelings Too?* by David L. Rice (Dawn Publications ©2000)
- *Feelings* by Aliki (HarperTrophy; Reprint edition ©1986)
- *Feelings: A First Poem Book About Feelings* by Felicia Law (Mercury Books ©2005)
- *The Feelings Book* by Todd Parr (Little, Brown Young Readers ©2005)
- *The Pigeon Has Feelings, Too!* by Mo Willems (Hyperion; Board edition ©2005)

Classroom Emotions Book: Bring in a digital camera. Take a variety of photos of the children. In each photograph the children should be signing a different emotion. Print out the photographs onto 8.5" x 11" (22 cm x 28 cm) paper. Place each photograph in a plastic sheet protector. Combine all of the photographs in a three ring binder to create a classroom scrapbook of emotions. The children will enjoy looking at the book and practicing the signs for all of the emotions.

Teach the Signed Phrases, How Do You Feel? and What's Wrong?: These signed phrases can be learned by the children but are mostly provided for the teacher to use. The teacher should become comfortable signing these phrases and teaching the children to recognize these phrases. The teacher can sign the question and the children can choose which emotion sign they would like to give in response.

I Love You: Parents will be delighted when the children go home and tell them "I love you" in sign.
Learn the Rhyme: Roses are red. Violets are blue. Do you love me? I love you. *(Sign the last line.)*

funny

The hand makes the letter "H" and taps the end of the nose.

happy

The open hand, with the palm facing the body, pats the heart in a circular motion.

How do you feel?

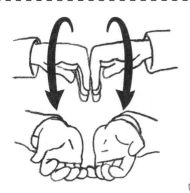

how

Point the fingers of both bent hands down and place the hands back to back. Revolve the hands in and upward together until the palms are flat and facing up.

you

The pointer finger is pointed straight ahead. This is a natural gesture for indicating a person.

feel

The middle finger moves several times up the chest.

I love you.

I love you.

Make the letter "Y" and hold up the pointer finger.

I

Point to yourself using the right pointer finger.

love

Fists cross at the wrist and then lay upon the chest.

you

The pointer finger is pointed straight ahead.

mad

The hand is held like a claw in front of the face and strikes down or in a circular motion.

sad

With both hands open, fingers apart and slightly bent, palms facing toward the face – move the hands down at the same time to mouth level.

sick

The right middle finger touches the forehead and the left middle finger touches the stomach. Make an ill-looking face.

scared

Both hands in fists, move quickly in front of the body as if to protect it. The hands open when they are in front of the body.

tired

The hands are placed on the chest and are moved downward along with the shoulders drooping to represent that someone does not have the strength to go on.

What's wrong?

The hand makes the letter "Y" and taps the chin.

Chapter Four

Colors

11 Signs to Be Learned: color, red, blue, yellow, green, orange, purple, brown, black, white, pink

(Reproduce the illustrated sign language cards found on pages 23–24. Make a copy for each child's "My Own Sign Language Dictionary," the Classroom Sign Word Wall, and one to be sent home to each child's parents.)

Getting Started: This chapter teaches the ASL signs for ten different colors. Most young children in early childhood programs are just learning to name and identify colors. The signs for colors are easy to learn for adults and older children who already know their colors and can read. The sign for the majority of the colors is the beginning consonant letter sign of the color word combined with a shaking motion of the hand. For example, to sign the color yellow, the right hand makes the letter "Y" and then the hand is shaken. However, for small children who are not yet reading, these signs can be difficult to learn and will require practice. When you are teaching a colors thematic unit, add the color signs as you introduce each individual color. An effective way to teach and compare colors in a preschool program is to present one new color each week.

Children's Literature: The following is a list of recommended children's books that may be used while teaching a unit on colors.

- *A Color of His Own* by Leo Lionni (Pantheon Books ©1975)
- *Babar's Book of Color* by Laurent De Brunhoff (Harry N. Abrams © New edition ©2004)
- *Brown Bear, Brown Bear, What Do You See?* by Bill Martin Jr. and Eric Carle (Henry Holt ©1996)
- *Cat's Colors* by Jane Cabrera (Puffin Books ©2000)
- *The Crayola Rainbow Colors Book* by Salina Yoon (Little Simon ©2004)
- *Mouse Paint* by Ellen Stoll Walsh (Red Wagon Books ©1995)
- *My Many Colored Days* by Dr. Seuss (Knopf Books for Young Readers ©1996)

Color Cans and the Illustrated Sign Language Cards: Copy, color, and cut out a set of the reproducible illustrated sign language cards found on pages 23–24. Laminate the cards for durability. Collect ten cans or plastic containers that come with plastic lids and then spray paint each container a different color. Most hardware stores carry spray paints that come in bright vivid colors and adhere well to plastic or metal. Paint these at home and wait to bring them to school until they are completely dry. Tape or glue each of the sign language cards to the bottom of each corresponding color can. For example, the sign language card for "red" is taped to the bottom of the "red" painted container.

These cans have two purposes. The first purpose is for the children to be able to self-check their own sign language practice. The children choose a container, make the sign for the color of that can, and then look at the bottom of the can to see of they made the correct sign.

The second purpose is for the children to sort colors. Provide the children with a large tub of small colorful counters, plastic toys, letters, and numbers. The children can sort the small objects by placing the toys in the containers according to color.

Colorful Cellophane: Colorful cellophane *(purchased at card or craft stores)* can create some exciting "color" discoveries for young children. Here is an assortment of activities that you can do with cellophane:

1. **Decorate Classroom Windows.** Colorful cellophane can be taped to window glass. The children will think it is fun to look through the window and see the world as "red" or "blue" or "green." You can create a stained-glass window by adding a new piece of cellophane to the window as you introduce each new color.
2. **Color Circles.** Place a piece of cellophane in an embroidery hoop. The children can look through the hoops or place different colored hoops on top of each other to create new colors.
3. **Cardboard Shape Frames.** Cut out shape frames from heavy cardboard. Tape the cellophane along the back of the frame. These can be used the same way as the embroidery frames, but are not as expensive.
4. **Cardboard Spyglasses.** Collect paper towel tubes and cover one end of the tube with cellophane. The children can pretend to be pirates and "spy" through the spyglass.

Colorful Clothespins: Paint wooden clothespins in a variety of colors. The clothespins can be used for sorting activities, for displaying the work of the children, or for actually hanging clothes. Put up a clothesline and provide the children with a basket of solid colored clothes or simply a basket of colored socks. The children can hang up the clothes with the matching colored clothespins.

This activity can also be turned into a game. The teacher can sign a color and the children should quickly hang up a piece of clothing of the signed color.

Brown Bear, Brown Bear, What Do You See? Classroom Big Book: *Brown Bear, Brown Bear, What Do You See?* is one of the best-loved children's books for teaching colors. As you read the book with the children, have them make the sign for each color instead of saying the color word. When you get to the end of the book the children might notice that there is not a pink animal. Have the children, as a group, write and color their own pink page for the book.

Create your own classroom big book with different animals. Write the story together as a class. The children might come up with *Pink Pig, Pink Pig, What Do You See?* The following pages might have purple cats, white bats, green dogs, black mice, or orange ants. Once you have decided on ten animals and their colors, divide the children into ten groups. Each group will be responsible for drawing and coloring a page for the classroom book. Provide each group with a large sheet of poster board, pencils, and crayons. Make sure that each child has an opportunity to color a section of their group's page. When completed, punch holes along the left side of each page and tie together to create a book. Read the book together as a class and remember to sign all of the colors!

Shaving Cream Colors: Place shaving cream in plastic bags that seal tightly. Add food coloring and watch the colors turn into new colors. Mix red and blue and discover purple. Mix yellow and red to discover orange. Mix blue and yellow to discover green.

Hopping on Colors: Place color squares on the floor. Make sure you have several squares of each color. Sign the colors to the children. For example, the teacher would point to a child and then sign the color "yellow" and then that child would hop on a yellow square. The children will delight in all the jumping and will quickly learn to recognize all of the colors and the signs for those colors.

Song—Who is Wearing (Color) Today? (Sung to the tune of "The Muffin Man"): Sing the following song but use signs for the colors.

Who is wearing (*color*) today?   (*Color*) today? (*Color*) today?
Who is wearing (*color*) today?   (*Child's name*) is wearing (*color*)!

Interactive Color Bulletin Board or Book:

Enlarge, copy, color, and cut out the illustrated sign language cards on pages 23–24. Laminate them for durability and place a piece of self stick Velcro® on the back of each card.

Place ten pieces of colored construction paper on a bulletin board or wall. Stick the corresponding piece of Velcro® on each of the ten pieces of colored paper. Let the children enjoy "sticking" the color sign language cards to the correct color of paper.

This activity can also be turned into an interactive book. Bind the ten pieces of construction paper together with yarn. The children can turn the pages and place the correct sign on each page.

color

Point the fingertips toward the mouth and wiggle them as the hand moves slightly forward.

red

The pointer finger strokes the lips.
(Lips are red.)

blue

The hand makes the letter "B" and shakes back and forth.

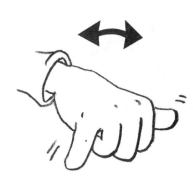

yellow

The hand makes the letter "Y" and shakes back and forth.

green

The hand makes the letter "G" and shakes back and forth.

orange
The open hand makes the letter "C" and is held at the mouth, then it squeezes as if squeezing an orange.

purple
The hand makes the letter "P" and shakes back and forth.

brown
The hand makes the letter "B" and slides down the side of the cheek.

black
The pointer finger draws a line across the forehead.

white
The hand makes a claw and is placed on the chest, and then it is pulled straight out with the fingertips coming together.

pink
The hand makes the letter "P" and strokes the lips.

· Chapter Five ·

Pets

---

7 Signs to Be Learned: bird, cat, dog, fish, mouse, pet, rabbit

(Reproduce the illustrated sign language cards found on pages 26–27. Make a copy for each child's "My Own Sign Language Dictionary," the Classroom Sign Word Wall, and one to be sent home to each child's parents.)

Getting Started: Animal signs are some of the most fun for children to learn. Some of these signs will even have the children pretending that they are an animal. Expect some lively fun when learning about pets in this chapter and farm animals in Chapter Six.

In this chapter the children will learn the sign for "pet" and the signs for six different pets: bird, cat, dog, fish, mouse, and rabbit.

Who Has a Pet and Who Doesn't: First find out how many of the children have a pet. Go around the room and ask the children if they have any pets. Make a list of all the different types of pets and the names of their pets. If a child does not have a pet, ask the child if there are any other family members who have a pet, such as an aunt, cousins, grandparents, or even a neighbor. Use the list of pet types and pet names for graphing activities. Count all the animals and turn it into a bar graph. How many dogs? How many cats? How many hamsters? How many fish? Make a column for each type of animal.

Then teach the children the sign for "pet."

Teach the Sign for Dog: This is a fun sign because it looks as if you are actually calling a dog. Dogs are perhaps the most popular of all the pets. They are people's best friend. Talk about some famous dogs: Lassie, Snoopy, 101 Dalmatians, just to name a few. Do the children have a favorite "famous" dog?
1. **Song – "How Much Is That Doggie in the Window?":** Make the sign for "dog" each time the word "doggie" appears in the song.
2. **Paper Plate Dog:** Give each child a small, dessert-size paper plate. Have the children glue on ears, draw facial features, and then attach a craft stick as a handle. Use the puppet when you sing "How Much Is That Doggie in the Window?".

Teach the Sign for Cat: The sign for "cat" makes one think of a cat's whiskers. There are many fun activities that can be used to teach the sign for "cat."
1. **Three Little Kittens:** Have the children memorize this rhyme and then dramatize it. Choose three children to be the kittens and use real mittens. Put one mitten on each child and hide the other three. Let all the children search for the mittens and match them to the correct child. Use the sign for "cat" each time the word "kittens" appears in the rhyme.
2. **Sing the Song "I Have a Little Cat" (Sung to the tune of "I'm a Little Teapot"):**

    I have a little cat.　　　　　　We play outside.
    Who's lots of fun.　　　　　　And, she chases me.
    When I call her, she always comes.　　I love my cat, and my cat loves me!

Teach the Sign for Bird: The children will make a pretend "beek" when they learn the sign for "bird."
1. **My Own Little Pet Bird:** Many children have birds as pets. Let each child make their own bird. Glue a small circle and a large circle together. Glue on some feathers (purchased at a craft store), and add wiggly eyes. Draw a picture of a nest on a piece of paper and glue the bird on the nest.

Teach the Sign for Fish: The children will delight as they move their hands as if they were two little fish swimming. Here are some fun activities to reinforce the sign for "fish."

1. **Fishing for Pets:** Make a fishing pole from a dowel rod. Attach a string with a magnet tied to the end. Make many fish cut-outs and tape a paper clip on each fish. Print numbers, colors, alphabet letters, or shapes on the fish. Let the children fish and then describe what they have caught. You can also glue pictures of pets on the cut-out fish. When the children "fish" out a pet, they must tell the class what they caught by "signing" what type of pet was caught.

2. **Four Little Fish:** Cut out four felt fish to be used on the flannel board. Have the children make the sign for "fish." Add the fish from the flannel board as directed by the rhyme:

   This first little fish loves to swim in the sun.   The fourth little fish likes to pretend he's a whale.
   The second little fish thinks diving is fun.   The four little fish are good friends.
   The third little fish made friends with a snail.   Now this rhyme has come to an end.

Teach the Sign for Mouse: Little mice often wiggle their nose–especially when they are sniffing for food. The sign for "mouse" draws attention to a sniffing nose.

1. **Hickory, Dickory, Dock:** Say the rhyme "Hickory, Dickory, Dock." Use the sign for "mouse." Add on to the rhyme. For example, "Hickory, Dickory Do. The mouse lost his shoe." or "Hickory, Dickory, Dee. The mouse skinned his knee." The children will think this is a lot of fun.

Teach the Sign for Rabbit: The children will look like little rabbits when they make the "rabbit" sign.

1. **Fluffy Rabbits:** Give each child a cardboard cut-out of a rabbit. Have the children "paint" diluted glue on the cut out and then fill the inside of the rabbit with cotton balls.

2. **Five Little Rabbits:** Learn the following rhyme and use the sign for "rabbit" when saying the rhyme. Make felt rabbits to be used on the flannel board.

   This little rabbit has two pink eyes.   This little rabbit is white as milk.
   This little rabbit is very wise.   This little rabbit nibbles away.
   This little rabbit is soft as silk.   He eats cabbage and carrots everyday.

Classroom Pet Show: Ask each of the children to bring a favorite stuffed animal to school. Have the children prepare to tell the class something about their stuffed pets. The children can even have the animals pretend to do tricks. Make blue ribbons. Be sure each pet gets a ribbon. Encourage the children to use the correct sign for each pet.

Classroom Pet Store: The stuffed animal pets can also be used in a creative play pet store learning center. Discuss all of the things that a pet would need in order to stay healthy.

Children's Literature: The following is a list of recommended children's books that may be used while teaching a unit on pets.

- *Arthur's Pet Business* by Marc Brown (Little Brown ©1993)
- *Bittle* by Patricia and Emily MacLachlan (Joanna Cotler ©2004)
- *Fish Is Fish* by Leo Lionni (Knopf ©1970)
- *How to Talk to Your Cat* by Jean Craighead George (HarperCollins ©2000)
- *How to Talk to Your Dog* by Jean Craighead George (HarperCollins ©2000)
- *I'll Always Love You* by Hans Wilhelm (Dragonfly Books ©1998)
- *Pet Show!* by Ezra Jack Keats (Puffin Books©2001)
- *Swimmy* by Leo Lionni (Knopf ©1963)

pet

With both hands flat, the fingertips of the right hand are brushed across the back of the left hand twice, as if one was stroking a pet.

bird

The pointer finger and thumb are held close to the mouth and then open and close like the beak of a bird.

cat

On both hands, the pointer fingers and the thumbs are pinched together with the remaining fingers standing tall. Then the thumbs and pointer fingers are placed on either side of the nose, and then pinched and pulled as if pulling whiskers.

dog

Slap your knee with your hand and then snap your fingers, as if calling a dog.

fish

The hands are open and make a swimming motion in front of the chest.

mouse

The pointer finger brushes past the nose.

rabbit

Both hands make the letter "U" and are held backwards on either side of the head. Then the fingers hop up and down just like a rabbit's ears.

Farm Animals

7 Signs to Be Learned: animal, chicken, cow, duck, horse, pig, sheep

(Reproduce the illustrated sign language cards found on pages 29–30. Make a copy for each child's "My Own Sign Language Dictionary," the Classroom Sign Word Wall, and one to be sent home to each child's parents.)

Getting Started: Chapter Six continues with more animal fun. In this chapter the children will learn about some farm animals and the signs for those animals. To begin the farm animal unit have the children sing, "Old MacDonald had a Farm." Let the children decide which animals will be added to each verse. After the children have learned the signs for the farm animals, have the children sing the song using the animal signs instead of the words.

What Do the Children Already Know About Farm Animals: If you teach in a rural setting, the young children in your classroom may already know a great deal about farm animals. Make a chart for each of the animals listed above. Write the children's comments on the charts and find pictures of these animals to add to the charts.

This activity is also a lot of fun for children who have only had city experiences. Teach the children the sign for "animal."

Teach the Sign for Chicken: Ask the children what they know about chickens. Do they know how chickens eat? The sign for "chicken" will mimic how a chicken eats.

1. **Sample Eggs:** Ask the children where eggs come from. Make hard-boiled eggs and serve them with butter and bread. Make a list of all the ways people can prepare eggs.

2. **Egg Carton Sort:** Collect several egg cartons. Color the bottom of each section a different color. Have the children sort small objects by color. Another carton can have numerals printed at the bottom of each section. The children can count out small objects and place them in the corresponding sections.

Teach the Sign for Cow: Teach the children the sign for "cow." Talk about how some cows have horns. The sign for "cow" might make the children think of horns.

1. **Dairy Delight:** Butter is fun to make! Every child will need a baby food jar or a container that will not leak. Pour whipping cream and a dash of salt into each jar (1/3 full). Seal tightly and have the children shake the jars. As the butter thickens, pour off the liquid into a large bowl. Serve the butter on bread. Talk about where dairy products come from. Brainstorm a list of some other dairy products.

Teach the Sign for Duck: This is a fun sign because it looks as if you are making the bill of a duck.

1. **Play "Duck, Duck, Cow" (Not "Goose" for This Game):** Have the children sit in a circle. Instead of saying, "Duck, Duck, Cow," have the person who is "it" sign the names of the animals. The first child who gets the sign "cow" must chase the child who is "it" around the circle.

2. **Sing the Song "Six Little Ducks":** Sing the song and let the children act out the song:
   Six little ducks went out to play, over the hill and far away.
   Mother duck said, "Quack, quack, quack."
   And five little ducks came waddling back.
   Five little ducks went out to play . . . and so on. Subtract a duck for each new verse.

Teach the Sign for Horse: All children seem to love horses. The sign for "horse" will remind the children of how a horse will perk up its ears when it is listening. Teach the children the following rhyme:

1. **If I was a Horse:**
   If I was a horse I would be big and brown.
   I would jump and run all over town.
   Leap on my saddle and don't look back.
   Because of course –I'm a very fast horse. *(Use the sign for "horse" instead of the word.)*

Teach the Sign for Pig: Ask the children if they can think of any famous pigs. How about the three pigs, Wilber from the book *Charlotte's Web*, or the movie star pig "Babe?" Teach the children the sign for "pig."

1. **Say the Rhyme "This Little Piggie Went to Market":** Use the sign for "pig" instead of the word.
2. **Stand-Up Pigs:** Give each child a small card stock cut out of a pig. Have the children paint the pigs and draw an eye and a nose. Use clothespins as legs so the pig can stand-up. Use these pigs when the children recite the above rhyme.

Teach the Sign for Sheep: Remind the children of some of the nursery rhymes that involve sheep, such as "Baa, Baa, Black Sheep," "Mary Had a Little Lamb," and "Little Boy Blue." Say the rhymes and then learn the sign for "sheep."

1. **Wooly Sheep:** Talk about all the things that are made from wool. Bring in several different types of wool for the children to touch.

Animal Cracker Fun: Give each child a small paper plate filled with animal crackers. Let the children sort the crackers according to the type of animal. (Save some crackers from the box to ensure a clean snack for snack time.) The animal crackers can also be glued on farm scenes drawn and colored by the children.

Animal Guessing Games: Give the children all sorts of clues and see if they can guess which animal you are talking about. Have the children answer in sign language.

1. I love the mud and have a curly tail. *(pig)*
2. I am very large and love to eat grass. I can give people all sorts of great food– especially ice cream. *(cow)*
3. People like to ride me. I am large and can help work on the farm. *(horse)*
4. I like to swim in ponds. Water seems to just run off my back. My mouth is called a bill. *(duck)*
5. I help people stay warm. I am very soft. *(sheep)*
6. I sit on a nest for long periods of time. I cluck. I have feathers. *(chicken)*

Let the children try to come up with their own clues for the animals.

Children's Literature: The following is a list of recommended children's books that may be used while teaching a unit on farm animals.

- *All the Places to Love* by Patricia MacLachlan (HarperCollins ©1994)
- *Click, Clack, Moo: Cows That Type* by Doreen Cronin (Simon & Schuster Children's Publishing ©2000)
- *Farming* by Gail Gibbons (Holiday House ©1990)
- *Giggle, Giggle, Quack* by Doreen Cronin (Simon & Schuster Children's Publishing ©2002)
- *Old MacDonald Had a Farm* by Carol Jones (Houghton Mifflin/Walter Lorraine Books ©1998)
- *Our Animal Friends at Maple Hill Farm* by Alice Provensen (Random House ©1984)

animal

The fingertips rest on the chest while the hands move back and forth. This motion represents the breathing motion of animals.

chicken

The right thumb and pointer finger mimic the action of a bird's beak. Then the right pointer finger scratches at the middle of the left palm (as if scratching for food.)

cow

The hand makes the letter "Y" and then the thumb is placed by the right temple and is turned back and forth to represent horns.

duck

The pointer and middle fingers tap the thumb in front of the mouth to mimic the movement of a duck's bill.

horse

Both hands make the letter "U" and are then placed on either side of the head and moved back and forth like the ears of a horse.

pig

The hand makes the letter "B" and is placed palm down under the chin and the fingers flap up and down as one.

sheep

Hold your left arm out in front of your body and have the right hand make the letter "V" (palm facing up). Move the right arm with the "V" fingers up and down the extended left arm as if shearing a sheep.

Chapter Seven

Food/Eating

> **18 Signs to Be Learned:** apple, banana, cookie, corn, cracker, drink, eat, hamburger, hungry, ice cream, lunch, milk, more, sandwich, snack, soup, thirsty, water
>
> *(Reproduce the illustrated sign language cards found on pages 33–35. Make a copy for each child's "My Own Sign Language Dictionary," the Classroom Sign Word Wall, and one to be sent home to each child's parents.)*

Getting Started: This chapter has eighteen signs that the children will be learning. Some of the signs are for words that are used throughout the day to express such needs as hunger and thirst. Some of the other signs are for foods that are commonly served at school during snack time and lunch. Because of the extensive number of signs that are taught in this chapter, a recommended outline is included. This outline lays out the order in which these eighteen signs can be most successfully presented.

Suggested Outline for the First Nine Signs: Drink, Eat, Hungry, Lunch, Milk, More, Snack, Thirsty, and Water.

1.   The first signs to be presented are "hungry" and then "eat." Introduce these signs right before lunch when you know the children are hungry. Be dramatic with the sign for "hungry." Who can make the "hungriest" sign? Then have the children sit down at the lunch table and then teach them the sign for "eat." "Eat" is one of the easiest signs for children to learn because it looks as if you are eating.

2.   The second group of signs to be presented are "thirsty" and "drink." Introduce these two signs in the same manner as you introduced "hungry" and "eat." Make sure the children really are "thirsty." After outdoor playtime is often a good time to introduce these signs.

3.   The third group of signs to be presented are "water" and "milk." Be sure that the children know the signs for "thirsty" and "drink" before you add "water" and "milk." At snack time, provide each of the children with a small glass of water and a small glass or milk. Tell the children they are going to play a game. Explain that when you sign "milk" the children may take a sip of milk. When you sign "water" the children may take a sip of water. You will be amazed at how quickly these signs are learned.

4.   The fourth group of signs are "lunch," "snack," and "more." Naturally, teach "lunch" at lunchtime and "snack" at snack time. A fun way to teach the sign "more" is to provide each child with a paper plate and just one animal cracker or one tiny apple slice. The children will be signing "more" almost immediately!

Suggested Outline for the Remaining Nine Food Signs: Apple, Banana, Cookie, Corn, Cracker, Hamburger, Ice Cream, Sandwich, and Soup.

1.   The first signs to be presented in this category are "apple" and then "banana." Most young children love these two fruits and eat them routinely. Give the children red and yellow play dough and have them mold a red apple and a yellow banana. Then practice these two signs.

2.   The second group of signs are four foods that are usually enjoyed by children and eaten at lunchtime: "corn," "hamburger," "sandwich," and "soup." Introduce these signs when the children are eating them. The tactile experience of the real food will make learning the sign easier.

3.   The final group of food signs to be presented are guaranteed to be the favorites, and they are "cookie," "cracker," and "ice cream." Before long the children will be signing "more ice cream."

Let's Go Grocery Shopping: Create a grocery store in your dramatic play learning area. Have shelves stocked with boxes and cans of food. Be sure that you have included all the foods that the children have been learning to sign, such as apple, banana, cookie, corn, cracker, hamburger, ice cream, milk, sandwich, soup, and water. Encourage the children to use the signs as they are playing.

Also have a cash register, play money, grocery bags, and if possible, shopping carts available for the children. Now, let the fun begin!

Make a Shopping List: Make picture cards (use the illustrated sign language cards) for each of the foods in the grocery store. Have the children use these cards to make a shopping list. The children choose the food cards they want and then they go to the store and purchase all the foods that are on their "shopping list."

Let's Go Out to Eat: Create a restaurant in your dramatic play learning area. Have several tables and chairs, a kitchen area to prepare the food, play food, aprons for the waiters and chefs, paper and pencils for taking orders, placemats, plates, cups, silverware (paper and plastic work well), trays for carrying the food to the customers, and menus. Encourage the children to use their signing vocabulary, including "please" and "thank-you."

Make Your Own Menus: Many restaurants have picture menus. They want their customers to see how "yummy" the food in the restaurant looks. Let the children design the menus for their restaurant. Provide the children with magazines and newspapers that have pictures of food. The children can cut out the food and then sort it by categories, such as all the desserts, all the meat dishes, all the fruits, all the beverages, etc. The children will enjoy this task and the menus will make a great addition to the classroom restaurant.

Build a Classroom Food Pyramid: On a bulletin board or wall, use masking tape to create the outline of the food pyramid. Let the children go through old magazines and newspapers and cut out pictures of food. Tape them to the food pyramid in their proper locations.

Stamping with Food: Use a variety of foods to create stamps. Potatoes, carrots, celery, apples, and cucumbers make excellent stamps. Cut the ends so one of the surfaces is flat. Dip the food in a small pan of tempera paint and then press onto paper.

Children's Literature: The following is a list of recommended children's books that may be used while teaching a unit on food and eating.
- *Bear Loves Food!* by Janelle Cherrington (Simon Spotlight ©1999)
- *The Berenstain Bears and Too Much Junk Food* by Stan Berenstain and Jan Berenstain (Random House Books for Young Readers ©1985)
- *Calling Doctor Amelia Bedelia* by Herman Parish (Greenwillow Press ©2002)
- *Doctor De Soto* by William Steig (Scholastic ©1986)
- *From Head to Toe* by Eric Carle (HarperTrophy ©1999)
- *Good Enough to Eat: A Kid's Guide to Food and Nutrition* by Lizzy Rockwell (HarperCollins ©1999)
- *Good Food* by DeMar Reggier (Scholastic Children's Press ©2006)
- *Where Does Food Come From?* by Shelley Rotner (Millbrook Press ©2005)

apple

The knuckle of the pointer finger is twisted by the side of the mouth. The cheek represents the apple and the knuckle represents the stem of the apple that is usually twisted out when someone eats an apple.

banana

The left pointer finger is held straight up (which represents the banana). The fingers of the right hand go around the pointer finger as if peeling the banana.

corn

The pointer finger is held across the front of the lower lip and turned as if eating an ear of corn.

cookie

One hand indicates the shape of a cookie in the palm of the other hand.

cracker

The motion of the hand and elbow indicates the breaking of a cracker.

drink

Tip an imaginary glass up to the mouth as if drinking.

eat

One hand pretends to place food in the mouth.

hamburger

The hands move as if making a hamburger patty.

hungry

The hand moves down the chest to indicate a desire for food to flow into one's stomach.

ice cream

One hand moves towards the mouth as if licking an ice cream cone.

lunch

The right elbow rests on the left hand (sign for noon) and then the right fingers touch the mouth (the sign for eat).

milk

The hand pretends to be milking a cow.

more

Both hands are held with the fingers touching (palms facing each other). Then the fingertips are tapped together.

sandwich

The hands are together with the fingertips pointing to the mouth, which represents a sandwich about to be eaten.

snack

The right pointer finger and thumb are pinched together and then moved to the mouth as if eating a bit of food.

soup

The right hand makes the letter "U" – representing a spoon which scoops up soup from a bowl formed by the left hand.

thirsty

The pointer finger draws a line down the throat to indicate that the throat is dry.

water

The hand makes the letter "W" and taps the chin.

Sign Language Fun in the Early Childhood Classroom

Chapter Eight

People

> **8 Signs to Be Learned:** boy, friend, girl, I/me, man, teacher, woman, you
>
> *(Reproduce the illustrated sign language cards found on pages 37–38. Make a copy for each child's "My Own Sign Language Dictionary," the Classroom Sign Word Wall, and one to be sent home to each child's parents.)*

Getting Started: This chapter will provide the children with eight of the signs for people. These signs will help the children when they are ready to sign phrases and will need words such as "you, me, and I." It also teaches the children the signs for "teacher, boy, girl, man, and woman"– words that are helpful in describing attributes.

It makes sense to introduce these eight signs in pairs: ("I/me" and "you"), ("girl" and "boy"), ("man" and "woman"), and finally ("friend" and "teacher").

Teach the Signs "I/Me" and "You": These are very simple signs to learn. One either points to "you" or "me."

The children will learn these quickly. To reinforce these concepts, have each of the children create a poster about themselves. The teacher should print at the top "All About Me!". The children should bring in a couple of personal photographs and then draw and color pictures of their favorites things. Some children might prefer to cut and paste pictures from magazines. The posters should reflect each child's own personality.

The teacher should also ask each child to answer this question: "What makes you special?" Record the answer and print "I am special because . . . " on the bottom of each child's poster.

Y-O-U Spells "You": Have the children play a version of Red Light/Green Light. The teacher stands in front of the children. Whenever she makes the sign "you," the children take two giant steps forward. When the teacher makes the sign "I," have the children take one tiny step backwards.

Who Is a Girl? Who Is a Boy?: Teach the children the signs for "girl" and "boy." Let the children make gingerbread "people" cookies. You can use a recipe or simply buy ready-made sugar cookie dough. Let the children use a "gingerbread person" cookie cutter to cut the shape from the dough. Provide the children with frosting, sprinkles, and raisins to decorate the cookies. The boys can decorate their cookies to look like boys and the girls can decorate their cookies to look like girls.

If you prefer not to bake, you can provide each of the children with a brown construction paper gingerbread person. Let the children decorate their gingerbread people with rickrack, crayons, glitter, sequins, buttons, yarn, markers, and anything else that could be helpful in turning the shapes into girls and boys.

 Sign Language Fun in the Early Childhood Classroom

Teach the Sign for Teacher: Teach the children the sign for "teacher." Set up a schoolroom in your dramatic play learning area. Place a blackboard on an easel with chalk, along with desks, chairs, paper, pencils, crayons, a school bell, a whistle for the teacher to use during recess, a map, a globe, and books for story time. Children will delight in pretending that they are the teacher.

My Mom Is a Woman, My Dad Is a Man: The next signs to be learned are "man" and "woman." Review with the children the signs for "girl" and "boy." The signs for "man" and "woman" begin with the sign for "girl" and "boy" and then add a second part to represent that the girl and boy have grown up. Ask the children to draw pictures of what they think they will look like when they grow up. Will they be tall? Will they be short? What will they be when they grow up?

Everyone Needs a Good Friend: Teach the children the sign for "friend." Everyone needs a special friend. Ask the children to talk about their special friends. What makes a good friend? What things do your friends do that make them good friends? Create a large bulletin board that is covered with all the comments from the children in your classroom about the importance of friendship. Ask the children to draw pictures of their friends.

Children's Literature: The following is a list of recommended children's books that may be used while teaching a unit on people.
- *All About Me* by Melanie Gerth (Piggy Toes Press ©2000)
- *Babies* by Gyo Fujikawa (Grosset & Dunlap ©1963)
- *Do You Want to Be My Friend?* by Eric Carle (HarperTrophy ©1987)
- *Guess How Much I Love You* by Sam McBratney (Candlewick Press ©1996)
- *A Splendid Friend, Indeed* by Suzanne Bloom (Boyds Mills Press ©2005)
- *Stand Tall, Molly Lou Melon* by Patty Lovell (GP Putnam's Sons ©2001)
- *Tell Me Something Happy Before I Go to Sleep* by Joyce Dunbar (Harcourt Children's Books ©1998)
- *Tell Me What It's Like to Be Big* by Joyce Dunbar. Harcourt Children's Books ©2001)
- *Will I Have a Friend?* by Miriam Cohen (Aladdin; Reprint edition ©1989)
- *Winnie-the-Pooh's Friendship Book* by A. A. Milne (Dutton Juvenile ©1994)

boy

The hand grasps the visor of a cap.

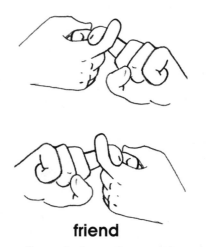

friend

The pointer fingers lock together, and then change positions and lock together in the opposite direction.

girl

The hand makes the letter "A" and then strokes the side of the chin. This represents the strings of a bonnet.

I / me

Point to yourself using the pointer finger.

man

The open hand with fingers and thumb extended touch the forehead and then touch the middle of the chest.

teacher

The fingertips of both hands are placed at the temples. Then the hands are swung out and move down the sides of the body.

woman

The hand is open with the fingers and thumb extended. The thumb touches the chin and then touches the chest.

you

The pointer finger is pointed straight ahead. This is a natural gesture for indicating a person.

Family

> **8 Signs to Be Learned:** baby, brother, dad, family, grandpa, grandma, mom, sister
> *(Reproduce the illustrated sign language cards found on pages 40–41. Make a copy for each child's "My Own Sign Language Dictionary," the Classroom Sign Word Wall, and one to be sent home to each child's parents.)*

Getting Started: Chapter Nine is all about families. This thematic unit is often one of young children's favorites. It is always fun to talk about the people we love. This unit also provides a good opportunity to review the sign for "pets" because many young children view their pets as family members. The children will notice some similarities with the signs "mom and grandma", "dad and grandpa," "girl" (from the previous chapter) and "sister," and "boy" (from the previous chapter) and "brother." Comparing the similarities of these signs will help the children to more easily remember them.

Teach the Sign for Family: Teach the children the sign for "family." Practice the sign several times and then lead the children in a discussion about families. Be sure to stress that there are many different kinds of family units (blended families, one-parent families, multi-generational families, extended families, foster families, adoptive families) and that all families are special. Have each of the children name all of the family members who live with them. Ask them what makes their families special. Have each child tell a "happy" story about their family.

Our Families Bulletin Board: Have each child draw and color a picture of all the people in their family. When the children have finished their pictures, ask each child to tell you who each person in the picture is. Write the names by each of the people in the pictures. Have the children count how many people are in their pictures. Make a family graph. Discuss the data. Who has the biggest family? The smallest family? Who has the most brothers? Sisters? How many of the children are the youngest in the family?

Teach the Sign for Baby: Show the children the sign for "baby" and then ask the children to guess what the sign means. You will probably hear the word "baby" shouted out. Ask each of the parents to send a baby picture of their child to school. Play a "baby guessing game." Show the pictures one at a time and have the children guess who the baby is. There will be many giggles! Ask the children to come up with a list of signs that they think a baby would need to know. Then ask the children to demonstrate what they think these signs would look like.

Teach the Signs for Brother and Sister: Compare how these signs are similar to the signs for "girl" and "boy." How many of the children have a brother or a sister? Make a list of what is fun about having siblings. What are some of the things that can make having a sibling a challenge? *(You will enjoy hearing these responses!)* Share one of the recommended books about brothers and sisters from the Children's Literature list on page 40.

 Sign Language Fun in the Early Childhood Classroom

Teach the Signs for Mom and Dad: Compare how these signs are similar. Let the children practice. Show the children several pictures of men and women (collected from storybooks or magazines). If you show a male picture the children should sign "dad." If you show a female picture the children should sign "mom." At first, show the pictures slowly and then increase the speed as the children become more secure with the two signs.

Teach the Signs for Grandma and Grandpa: Compare how these signs are similar to the signs for "mom" and "dad." Let the children practice. Teach the children the rhyme, "These are Grandma's Glasses." The first time say the rhyme with the word "grandma." The second time say it with the word "grandpa."

These are grandma's glasses.	These are grandpa's glasses.
This is grandma's cap.	This is grandpa's hat.
This is the way she folds her hands	This is the way he folds his hands
And lays them in her lap.	And lays them in his lap.

Family Scrapbook: Ask the children's parents to send 4 to 6 family photographs to school. Let the children make a family scrapbook page for each of the photos. The children can decorate them with stickers, drawings, sequins, glitter, and whatever craft items that you have on hand. Have the children make a cover for their family scrapbook and then place each page in a sheet protector. Use brads to bind the pages together to form a book. These books make great holiday gifts for parents or grandparents.

Play House: Encourage the children to use the signs for family members when the children are playing house in the home living learning center.

Children's Literature: The following is a list of recommended children's books that may be used while teaching a unit on families.
- *All Families Are Different* by Sol Gordon and Vivien Cohen (Prometheus Books ©2000)
- *Are You My Mother?* by P.D. Eastman (Random House Books for Young Readers ©1960)
- *The Best Worst Brother* by Stephanie Stuve-Bodeen (Woodbine House ©2005)
- *Clifford's Family* by Norman Bridwell (Scholastic ©1984)
- *Hooray for Grandparents Day!* by Nancy Carlson (Puffin ©2002)
- *I Want a Brother or Sister* by Astrid Lindgren (Farrar Straus & Giroux ©1988)
- *That's What Grandparents Are For* by Arlene Uslander (Peel Productions ©2001)
- *The Wednesday Surprise* by Eve Bunting (Clarion Books ©1989)
- *Who's in a Family?* by Robert Skutch and Laura Nienhaus (Tricycle Press ©1997)

baby

Arms are held as if cradling a baby and rocking it back and forth.

brother

The hand, palm down, is held at the forehead. The fingers open and close a few times. Then, with one movement, both pointer fingers point forward and are brought together

dad

The thumb of the open hand touches the forehead.

family

Both hands make the letter "F" with the palms facing away from the body. Then the hands are swung out in opposite directions and circled in front until the fingers touch.

grandpa

The thumb of the open hand touches the forehead and then the hand moves out in small arcs.

grandma

The thumb of the open hand touches the chin and then the hand moves out in small arcs.

mom

Touch the chin with the thumb of your open hand.

sister

The hand makes the letter "A" and strokes the side of the cheek. Then in one movement, both pointer fingers point forward and are brought together.

Chapter Ten

Weather

> **6 Signs To Be Learned:** cloud, cold, hot, rain, snow, sun
>
> *(Reproduce the illustrated sign language cards found on page 44. Make a copy for each child's "My Own Sign Language Dictionary," the Classroom Sign Word Wall, and one to be sent home to each child's parents.)*

Getting Started: Weather is a topic that is discussed daily in early childhood classrooms. Children talk about if it is "cold" or "hot" outside. Is the sun shining? Are there clouds? Is there snow or rain? The children also talk about dressing properly for the weather.

Teach the Signs for Hot and Cold: Teach the children the signs for "hot" and "cold." Have the children practice these new signs using the rhyme, "Peas Porridge Hot."

Pease porridge hot.	Some like it hot.
Pease porridge cold.	Some like it cold.
Pease porridge in the pot.	Some like it in the pot.
Nine days old.	Nine days old.

Play the Game "Hot or Cold": Show the children a small toy. Then choose one child to be "it." "It" should step out of the room while the teacher (or another child) hides the small toy somewhere in the classroom. "It" comes back into the room and begins searching for the toy. The other children sign "cold" if the child is far away from the hidden toy. The children should sign "hot" when the child is getting close to the hidden toy.

Play Hot Potato: Have the children sit in a circle and begin passing a small bean bag around the circle. The children should pass the bean bag quickly because they are pretending that the bean bag is a "hot potato." The teacher starts the game by signing "hot." That signals the children to begin passing the potato. When the teacher suddenly signs "cold" all the children should stop passing the potato. The child who is holding the potato gets to take the teacher's place and sign "hot" to begin the game and then "cold" to stop the action.

Teach the Sign for Sun: Teach the children the sign for "sun." Give each child a small paper plate and have them paint their plates bright yellow. Sprinkle gold glitter on the plate while the paint is still wet. After the plate is completely dry have the children glue on a yarn smile and a pair of black construction paper sunglasses. Now practice the sign for "sun."

Sun Smoothies and Sunny Popsicles: Fill a blender with orange juice, several strawberries, and some ice cubes. Blend well and serve in small paper cups. The is a very healthy "sunny" beverage. Also fill ice cube trays with lemonade and place a craft stick in each section. Freeze, then serve and enjoy!

Teach the Sign for Cloud: Teach the children the sign for "cloud." On a nice warm (and cloudy) day take the children outside, have them lay down on the grass, and study the clouds. What do they see? Encourage the children to use their imaginations. Go back into the classroom and give the children blue construction paper, glue, and cotton balls or batting. Ask them to recreate one of the clouds that they saw outside.

Teach The Sign for Rain: Teach the children the sign for "rain." Have the children say the following rhymes and use the signs for "rain" and "sun" as the words appear in each rhyme:

The Eency, Weency Spider
The eency weency spider climbed up the water spout.
Down came the rain and washed the spider out.
Out came the sun and dried up all the rain.
Now the eency weency spider climbs up the spout again.

Rain, Rain, Go Away
Rain, rain, go away.
Come again another day.
Little (*child's name*)
Wants sun today.

Rain Pictures: Have each of the children color an outdoor picture. They might choose to color the playground or the fronts of their houses. When the children are done with their pictures, have them "carefully" drip white drops of glue all over their work. When the glue dries, it will look just like rain.

Rain in the Classroom: How exciting to make it rain in the classroom! Fill a tea kettle with water and bring it to a boil. Hold an empty jar over the spout of the kettle. The jar will fill with steam (*which looks like a cloud*), and because the jar is cool, the steam inside the jar will form droplets and then drip down just like rain!

Teach the Sign for Snow: Teach the children the sign for "snow." Bring in a pan of snow or fill the water table with snow. This is especially fun if you live in a warm climate. (*Snow can be made from an inexpensive snow cone machine.*) Let the children use kitchen utensils and cookie cutters while they dig in the snow and make tiny snowmen and small igloos.

Snow Experiments: First, bring some snow into the classroom or get ice crystals from inside a freezer. Look at them under a magnifying glass. How many points does a snowflake have? Then, melt snow and ice in a pan. Will they both turn into water?

Marshmallow Snow People: Build snowpeople by using a small amount of white glue to glue two or three large marshmallows together. Use scrap fabric for a scarf; toothpicks for arms; and draw on a face with fine-lined magic markers.

Play Dough Snow People: Make snowmen with a commercially manufactured light-weight "white" modeling compound that air dries and can be painted. As an alternative, you can use this homemade play dough recipe: 1 cup (240 mL) salt; 2 cups (470 mL) flour; 6 teaspoons (30 mL) alum; 2 tablespoons (30 mL) vegetable oil; and 1 cup (240 mL) water. Mix together.

Children's Literature: The following is a list of recommended children's books that may be used while teaching a unit on weather.
- *I Love You, Sun, I Love You, Moon* by Karen Pandell and Tomie dePaola (Putnam ©1994)
- *Little Cloud* by Eric Carle (Putnam ©2001)
- *The Mitten* by Jan Brett (Putnam Publishing Group ©1989)
- *On Mother's Lap* by Ann Herbert Scott (Clarion Books ©1992)
- *Polar Bear, Polar Bear, What Do You Hear?* by Bill Martin Jr. and Eric Carle (Henry Holt & Co. ©1997)
- *Rain* by Robert Kalan (HarperTrophy ©1991)
- *Rain Drop Splash* by Alvin Tresselt (HarperTrophy ©1990)
- *The Snowman* by Raymond Briggs (Random House Children's Publishing ©1998)
- *Sun Up, Sun Down* by Gail Gibbons (Voyager Books ©1987)
- *The Tomten* by Astrid Lindgren (Putman Juvenile ©1997)

cold

The shoulders are hunched forward and the hands shake as if the signer is cold.

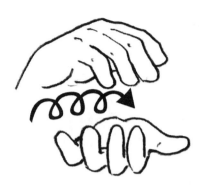

cloud

Both hands held in claw shapes swirl around with palms facing each other.

hot

The hand is held in a claw shape and is facing the mouth, and then the hand turns out quickly as if throwing something away.

rain

The fingers of both hands are spread and bent. The hands move down to represent the falling rain.

snow

The fingers wiggle as the hands move down to represent snowflakes falling.

sun

The pointer finger points to the sky and circles to indicate the shape of the sun. The hand is then turned towards the head and the fingers spreadout to represent the sun shining down from the sky.

Toys

7 Signs To Be Learned: ball, block, book, game, play, puppet, toy
(Reproduce the illustrated sign language cards found on pages 46–47. Make a copy for each child's "My Own Sign Language Dictionary," the Classroom Sign Word Wall, and one to be sent home to each child's parents.)

Getting Started: Chapter Eleven is a thematic unit about toys. The children will learn the sign for "play," along with the signs for six of the most popular free-time activities for children.

Teach the Sign for Play: Teach the children the sign for "play." Have the children brainstorm a list of their favorite play activities. Read the list back to the children and then have them sign "play" and read one of the ideas from the play list.

Teach the Sign for Ball: Before you show the children the sign for "ball," ask them what they think a good sign for the word "ball" would be. Did any of the children guess the correct sign? The following two activities will help reinforce the concept of the sign for "ball."

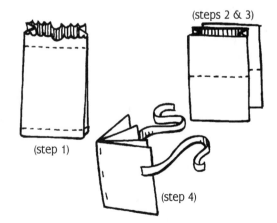

Catch-a-Ball: The children should each have a plastic cup, a piece of string, and a large bead (ball). Lace the bead onto the string and tie a knot at the end of the string (see illustration). The teacher should cut a small slit in the plastic cup. Place approximately 2" (5 cm) of the string through the slit and tape the end to the inside of the cup. The objective is to swing the bead (ball) and try to catch it in the cup.

Ball Bouncing Contest: Bouncing a ball is a difficult gross motor skill for a young child. Take the children outside and let them practice "bouncing." Count how many times each child can bounce the ball without stopping or having the ball "bounce away."

Teach the Sign for Book: Teach the children the sign for "book." Take the children to the school library and let them each check out a favorite book.

Shape Book: Create a shape on one piece of paper. Staple it onto three or four other pieces of paper and then cut through all the thicknesses. Staple the shapes together to complete the shape book.

Paper Bag Book: Use two lunch-size paper bags. Cut off the bottom of each one and trim off the tops (step 1). Glue the bottom and top openings closed to make flat booklet pages (steps 2 & 3). Stack the two bags on top of one another and then fold them in half the short way. Staple along the fold. Glue 6" (15 cm) pieces of ribbon to the front and back flaps (step 4). Tie the ribbons together to keep the book closed.

(steps 2 & 3)

(step 1)

(step 4)

Teach the Sign for Block: Teach the children the sign for "block." Show the children the sign and ask them what they think this sign could represent.

Wood Blocks: Commercial wood blocks can be very expensive. You can create your own wooden blocks by using scrap lumber. Have the wood cut to appropriate sizes for the children to manipulate. The blocks must be sanded well to prevent splinters.

Make Your Own Blocks: Building blocks are an essential toy for children to play with, discover, and explore during their early childhood years. Children can increase gross motor skills, spacial skills, vocabulary, and imagination when they play with blocks. Here are some ideas for making your own inexpensive blocks: Collect half gallon milk cartons, half-and-half cartons, and small individual school milk cartons. Wash well, rinse, and allow to completely dry. Fold in and tape down the top of each carton so you have created a rectangle. Cover each of the cartons with decorative "shelf-lining" contact paper. Collect as many cartons as possible so the children can build palaces, forts, and castles.

Teach the Sign for Game: Teach the children the sign for "game." Have the children play some of the following games:

Decorate the Clown: Cut a large clown shape from pellon and draw on facial features. Decorate the clown's clothes with various shapes. Draw each shape in a different color. Cut out corresponding felt shapes. For example, if there is a red circle drawn on the clown there should be a red felt circle cut out. The children can match the felt shapes to the outlines on the clown's clothes.

Matching Textures: Collect scrap fabrics that include a variety of textures: velvet, dotted-swiss, burlap, cotton, silk, nylon, and wool. Using pinking shears, cut two swatches from each fabric and store them in a bag. The children can then reach into the bag and try to discover matching fabrics simply by the way that they feel.

Teach the Sign for Puppet: Teach the children the sign for "puppet." Puppets are wonderful toys for increasing language skills. Encourage the children to play with puppet and to create their own puppet shows.

Puppets: Paper bags, paper plates, and socks can create wonderful puppets. Keep a box of craft materials available for the children to use for decorating their puppets. Stick puppets can be made by cutting out pictures from coloring books, magazines, and catalogs. Tape the cutouts to tongue depressors or craft sticks.

Teach the Sign for Toy: Teach the children the sign for "toy."

Toy-Matching: Divide a large sheet of poster board into 12 sections. Then make two identical sets of twelve toy picture cards. Use coloring books, toy catalogs, magazines, or take pictures of toys in your home to make these cards.

Glue or tape one set of pictures on the poster board and then cover the board in clear contact paper. The other set of pictures can be taped onto index cards and used as playing cards. The children should take the playing cards and match them to the identical toy on the poster board.

Children's Literature: The following is a list of recommended children's books that may be used while teaching a unit on toys.
- *Curious George Visits a Toy Store* by H. A. Rey (Houghton Mifflin ©2002)
- *Max's Toys* by Rosemary Wells (Viking ©2004)
- *The Toy Cupboard* by David Wood (Piggy Toes Press ©2000)

play

Both hands make the letter "Y" and twist back and forth at the same time.

ball

Both hands are open and the fingertips touch and tap while making the shape of a ball.

block

The right fingertips tap the open left palm above the wrist, and then the left hand fingertips tap the right open palm above the wrist.

book

Both hands open and close with the little fingers making the spine of the book.

game

Both hands make the letter "A" with the knuckles touching each other and then the thumbs are wiggled.

puppet

The pointer fingers and thumbs touch and then move up and down as if manipulating marionettes.

toy

Both hands make the letter "T" and twist back and forth at the same time.

Chapter Twelve

School Tools

---

6 Signs to Be Learned: crayon, glue, paint, pencil, paper, scissors

(Reproduce the illustrated sign language cards found on page 50. Make a copy for each child's "My Own Sign Language Dictionary," the Classroom Sign Word Wall, and one to be sent home to each child's parents.)

Getting Started: The most common school tools are crayons, glue, paint, pencil, paper, and scissors. These are typically the first "tools" that children learn to use in school. This unit will teach the children the signs for these objects and provide age-appropriate activities for fine motor practice.

Teach the Sign for Crayon: Teach the children the sign for "crayon." The following are some fun "crayon" activity ideas:

Solid Color Crayons: Fill a sauce pan with 2½" (6 cm) of water. Take an empty tin can and "pinch" the top to create a pouring spout. Set the can in the water. Using medium heat, bring the water to a boil. Fill ¼ of the can with broken crayons of the same color. Once the crayons have melted, pour the melted crayon wax into paper cupcake liners that have been placed in a cupcake tin. Let the wax cool completely before removing the cupcake liners. Now the children can color with their own homemade crayons!

Homemade Rainbow Crayons: Fill each muffin tin, cupcake tin, or even a candy mold with broken crayons. To make rainbow crayons, place four to five different colored broken crayon pieces in each section. Place in a 400° oven just long enough for the crayons to melt. Watch them carefully, as crayons melt very quickly. If you leave the crayons in the oven too long, the colors will blend together. You want the crayons to become soft–not liquid. Take the pan out of the oven and place it on a cooling rack. After cooling, pop out the crayons and enjoy coloring!

Teach the Sign for Glue: Teach the children the sign for "glue."

Smelly Glue: Pour a small amount of white glue into several paper cups. Add some drink mix powder or Kool-Aid® powder. This activity is even more fun if you have several different flavors available. The children can paint the "flavored" glue onto paper or a paper plate. (Make some of the drink mix so the children can taste what they are seeing and smelling.) Let them touch the glue when it is dry. Have them smell their fingers. Did the scent rub onto their fingertips?

Make Your Own Colored Glue: Don't throw away those old markers! Place them in a bowl of water and let them soak until you see the water starting to turn color. Place the soaked markers in separate bottles of glue and let them soak overnight. By the next day you will have bottles of colored glue. The children can use the glue just like puff paint, squeezing it and creating designs on a piece of paper. The children will have fun tracing their fingers over the smooth glue lines when the art is dry.

Teach the Sign for Paint: Teach the children the sign for "paint."

Soapy Flakes Paint: Using an electric mixer, beat Ivory Snow® and water together until a creamy mixture is formed. Keep the soap flakes white and finger paint on a dark-colored piece of paper. Use this paint while freshly whipped. Then add color to the mixture and keep on painting.

Puffy Paint: Mix equal parts of flour, salt, and water together in a bowl. Add tempera paint for color. Mix well and pour into a squeeze bottle that has a narrow nozzle. Squeeze the puffy paint onto cardboard or a heavy stock paper. The paint mixture will become hard as it dries.

Teach the Sign for Pencil: Teach the children the sign for "pencil." Here are some teaching tips that will help your young students learn how to use a pencil:

Pencil Grips: Use pencil grips for children who have a difficult time remembering how to hold their pencil.

Short Pencils: Break or sharpen pencils down to about a 2" (5 cm) length. This will encourage small hands to hold the pencil properly.

Chubby Writing Tools: Use sidewalk chalk, chubby crayons, or a chubby pencil cut down to a short 2"(5 cm) length to help children gain more control.

Slanted Surface: Learning how to print is easier when children are permitted to work on a slanted surface. Place a 4" (10 cm) three ring-binder on the desk in front of the child. The spine of the binder should be facing the top of the desk. Rotate the binder to a 45 degree angle. Tape a piece of writing paper on the binder. Writing on this slanted surface is fun and can be extremely beneficial for learning to print.

Teach the Sign for Paper: Teach the children the sign for "paper."

Colorful Tissue Paper: Tear the tissue paper into small shapes and set them aside. Mix 2 parts glue and 1 part water in a paper cup. Paint this diluted glue onto a piece of white construction paper. Pick up the tissue paper, one piece at a time, and place the shapes all over the wet glue. The variety of colors and the various shapes of the tissue paper will make for some interesting designs. When the paper is dry, you can brush the diluted glue over the tissue paper again to create a smooth "varnished" finish.

Torn Paper Pictures: Give the children a variety of colored construction paper. Have the children tear the paper into small pieces and then have them glue the small paper pieces into an interesting design on another piece of construction paper.

Teach the Sign for Scissors: Teach the children the sign for "scissors."

Snipping Funny Shapes: Let the children enjoy cutting shapes out of colored construction paper. It does not matter how big or what shapes the pieces are. The teacher should cut out and remove the backing on an 8.5" x 11" (22 cm x 28 cm) piece of contact paper. When each child has a small pile of colored shapes, they can simply "stick" the shapes on the contact paper. When finished, the contact paper can be turned over and stuck to another sheet of paper. The result is a work of scissor art ready for display.

Scissor Cutting Magazines and Catalogs: This simple activity is very educational and is also an activity that children will enjoy doing for long periods of time. Simply provide children with magazines or catalogs and let them cut out pictures and glue them onto paper using glue sticks. This activity can also help children learn how to categorize and sort. Have the children cut out pictures and sort them into specified categories, such as people, furniture, clothes, or food.

School Tools Rhyme: Have the children learn the following rhyme and use the new "school tools" signs as they recite it:

Pencils and paper.	Crayons to color.	These are tools.
Paint and Glue.	Scissors too.	We use at school.

Children's Literature: The following is a list of recommended children's books that may be used while teaching a unit on school and school tools.

- *Clifford's First Day at School* by Norman Bridwell (Scholastic ©1999)
- *Harold and the Purple Crayon 50th Anniversary Edition* by Crockett Johnson (HarperTrophy ©1981)
- *If You Take A Mouse to School* by Laura Numeroff (Laura Geringer ©2002)
- *I Love You All Day Long* by Francesca Rusackas (HarperCollins ©2002)
- *Miss Bindergarten Gets Ready for Kindergarten* by Joseph Slate (Dutton Children's Books ©1996)
- *Mouse Paint* by Ellen Stoll Walsh (Voyager Books ©1995)
- *What to Expect at Preschool* by Heidi Murkoff (HarperFestival ©2001)

crayon

The open right hand touches the lips (sign for color)
and then pretends to color on the left palm.

glue

The right hand makes the letter "G" and then
pretends to drip glue on the left palm.

paint

The right hand makes a letter "B" with the thumb
extended and then pretends to be a paintbrush
and brushes "paint" on the left palm.

pencil

The tips of the
pointer finger
and thumb touch,
and then touch the
lips as if licking the
tip of a pencil.
The fingertips then
pretend to write
on the left palm.

paper

Both open flat
hands brush
against each
other twice in
front of the chest.

scissors

The pointer finger and middle finger
show the action of scissors.

Chapter Thirteen

Everyday Objects

> **8 Signs To Be Learned:** chair, coat, door, flower, hat, shoes, table, window
>
> *(Reproduce the illustrated sign language cards found on pages 52–53. Make a copy for each child's "My Own Sign Language Dictionary," the Classroom Sign Word Wall, and one to be sent home to each child's parents.)*

Getting Started: The everyday objects presented in this chapter are a springboard to help you get started teaching signs of items commonly recognized by young children. A "door" and "window" are found in everyone's home; "tables" and "chairs" are seen everywhere; all children wear "shoes," "coats," and "hats," and the sign for "flower" is simply fun! Let the children come up with a list of other everyday signs that they would like to learn.

Teach the Signs for Window and Door: Teach the children the sign for "window" and "door." When you demonstrate the signs for the children they may think that you are signing the word "open" because it looks as if you are "opening" a window or a door. Here are some fun ideas to help reinforce the learning of these new signs.

Window Paint: To begin, use tape and newspaper to protect the walls and flooring. Mix liquid dish washing soap into tempera paint to help make the paint removal easier. Then let the children create a window masterpiece. Special Note: The longer the window paint is left on a window, the harder it will be to remove. As an alternative, you can cover the window with cellophane and paint on the cellophane instead.

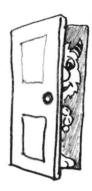

What's Behind the Door?: Read *There's a Nightmare in My Closet* by Mercer Mayer to the children. Have the children sign the word for "door" each time you read the word "closet." After reading the story, have each child glue along the left side of a brown piece of construction paper (door) onto a piece of white paper. Fold the paper back so that the door can open and close. Have the children draw and color surprises behind their doors.

Teach the Signs for Table and Chair: Teach the children the signs for "table" and "chair." Here are some fun activities to help the children learn the new signs:

A Chair for My Mother: This heart-warming story is about a girl, her mother, and grandmother who save their money to buy a big rose-colored comfortable chair after everything they owned was lost in a fire. Have the children draw and color what they believe would be the world's best chair. What color is their chair? How big is their chair? Use the sign for "chair" during this activity.

Table Top Painting: Cover the tabletop with finger painting paper. Make some instant pudding and let the children have fun finger painting with this yummy texture.

Teach the Signs for Shoes, Coat, and Hat: Teach the children the signs for "shoes," "coat," and "hat." Here are some fun ideas to help the children remember these new signs:

Shoes: Read any version of *The Elves and the Shoemaker.* Set up a cobbler play area and let the children pretend to be elves. The children will also enjoy playing "find the match." Have all the children take off one shoe. Put all of the shoes in a pile. As soon as the teacher signs "shoes" the children should run to the pile and grab a shoe. Be sure to tell them NOT to grab their own shoes. Then have the children look at each other's feet to find the person who owns the shoe they are holding.

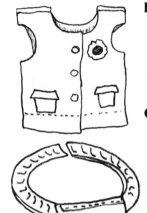

Fashion Designers: Ask the parents to send a pillowcase to school for their child. The teacher should cut armholes, a slit up the front, and an opening for the head (*see illustration*). The children can turn the pillowcase into a fancy new coat by using fabric crayons, fabric paint, or puff paint, along with gluing on sequins or other adornments. This activity can also be done with brown grocery bags.

Create Matching Visors: Children love wearing visors and they are easy to make. You will need a paper plate and a half for each child. Have each child color and decorate the half paper plate and edges of the whole paper plate. Once the pieces are completed, the teacher should cut off the rim of the whole plate approximately 1½" (4 cm) wide. Staple the half plate to the rim of the other plate (see illustration). Cover the staples with masking tape to protect the child's head. Measure the visors to the children's heads to ensure that they fit and tape the ends together.

Teach the Sign for Flower: Teach the children the sign for "flower." To help the children learn this sign let them have the fun of operating a flower shop in the dramatic play area of the classroom.

Flower Shop: Ask the parents to donate artificial flowers. Large cups and play dough work well for flower arranging. Place the play dough in the bottom of a cup and let the children push the flower stems into the dough. Add ribbons and other fun touches to finish the arrangements.

Real Flowers: Teddy Bear sunflowers are great fun to grow. They germinate easily and they are a hearty flower to begin growing in a classroom. They are also easy to transplant into an outside flower garden. (Not to mention that children love the name of this flower.)

Children's Literature: The following is a list of recommended children's books that may be used while teaching a unit on everyday objects.
- *A Chair for My Mother* by Vera B. Williams (Greenwillow ©1982)
- *Flower Garden* by Eve Bunting (Voyager Books ©2000)
- *Kenny's Window* by Maurice Sendak (Michael Di Capua ©2002)
- *The Kettles Get New Clothes* by Dayle Ann Dodds (Candlewick ©2002)
- *The Little House* by Virginia Lee Burton (Houghton Mifflin ©1978)
- *Richard Scarry's Best First Book Ever!* by Richard Scarry (Random House ©1979)
- *There's a Nightmare in My Closet* by Mercer Mayer (Dial ©1968)

chair

The right hand pointer and middle fingers are placed on top of the left hand pointer and middle fingers (sign for "sit") which are then tapped twice to represent sitting on a chair.

coat

Both hands make the letter "A" and then, as if holding the sides of a coat, pull down from the collar to the waist.

door

Both hands make the letter "B" facing forward with the thumbs touching. Both hands push forward and the right hand swings open like a door.

flower

The hand makes a flattened "O," and then the fingertips move under the nose as if smelling flowers.

hat

The open right hand taps the top of the head.

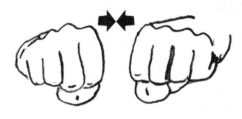

shoes

Both hands make the letter "A" and are tapped together to represent a person clicking the heels of their shoes.

table

Both hands and arms are flat with the right arm resting on the left arm – as if resting on a table.

window

Both hands make the letter "B" with the right hand resting on top of the left hand and palms facing the body. Then the hands are pulled apart as if opening a window.

Chapter Fourteen

Numbers

> **21 Signs To Be Learned:** zero, one, two, three, four, five, six, seven, eight, nine, ten, eleven, twelve, thirteen, fourteen, fifteen, sixteen, seventeen, eighteen, nineteen, twenty
>
> *(Reproduce the illustrated sign language cards found on pages 56–58. Make a copy for each child's "My Own Sign Language Dictionary," the Classroom Sign Word Wall, and one to be sent home to each child's parents.)*

Getting Started: The illustrated reproducible sign language cards have been provided for the numbers zero through twenty. It is up to the individual classroom teacher to decide how many numbers the children are ready to learn. Teachers in classrooms of young preschool children may only want to introduce numbers one, two and three. Kindergarten teachers may wish to introduce all of the provided numbers. The following ideas will get you started and may be adapted to a wide range of numbers.

Teach the Number Signs Appropriate for the Age and Ability of the Students: Enlarge, copy, cut out and laminate for durability the illustrated sign language number cards found on pages 56–58. Put up a clothesline in your classroom. On wooden clothespins, print with a black permanent marker the numbers zero through twenty. Each time you introduce a number to the children bring out the card and add it to the clothesline. Use this activity to provide daily number review, and to let the children have the fun of sequencing the numbers, and for matching the clothespins to the correct number cards.

      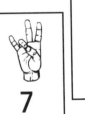 

More Clothespin Number Fun: The teacher will need to have clothespins with numbers written on them for both of the following activities.

Clothespin Wheel—Numbers One to Ten
Print numbers around the edge of a paper plate. Then print numbers on the wooden clothespins. The children can then attach the numbered clothespins next to the matching number on the plate.

Clothespin Can—Numbers
Draw sets of numbers along the top edge of a can. If you cannot print directly onto the can, draw the number sets on paper and then glue the paper to the can. You can also create the sets by using stickers. Have the children attach the numbered wooden clothespins above the corresponding sets of numbers along the top of the can.

Wonderful Rhymes: Rhymes are one of the best ways to help young children learn to count and to practice the number signs. Teach the children some of the following rhymes and encourage them to sign the numbers. These rhymes will provide hours of educational fun!

Ten Silly Elephants

Ten silly elephants standing in a line–
One ran away, and then there were nine.
Nine silly elephants standing at the gate–
One went for hay, and then there were eight.

Eight silly elephants counting to eleven–
One saw a mouse, and then there were seven.
Seven silly elephants picking up sticks–
One built a house, and then there were six.

Six silly elephants looking at a hive–
One chased a bee, and then there were five.
Five silly elephants dancing on the floor–
One bumped his knee, and then there were four.

Four silly elephants sitting in a tree–
One fell out, and then there were three.
Three silly elephants wearing something blue–
One gave a shout, and then there were two.

Two silly elephants sitting in the sun–
One went swimming, and then there was one.
One silly elephant looking for some fun–
Went to join the circus, and then there was none!

(Flannel Board Fun: Enlarge the elephant pattern. Make ten copies on gray card stock. Place a piece of self-stick Velcro® on the back of each elephant. Place all ten elephants in a line on the flannel board. Remove the elephants as directed by the rhyme.)

Engine, Engine, Number Nine

Engine, engine, number nine
Running on Chicago Line,
Please tell me the correct time.
One o'clock, two o'clock,
Three o'clock, four o'clock,
Five o'clock, six o'clock,
Seven o'clock, eight o'clock. Nine!

Three Men in a Tub

Rub a dub, dub,
Three men in a tub
And who do you
Think they be?
The butcher, the baker,
The candlestick maker,
Toss them out–all three.

Two Little Blackbirds

Two little blackbirds,
Sitting on the hill.
One named Jack.
One named Jill.
Fly away, Jack.
Fly away, Jill.

Come back, Jack.
Come back, Jill.
Two little blackbirds,
Sitting on the hill.
One named Jack.
One named Jill.

Ten Little Fingers

I have ten little fingers and ten little toes.
Two little arms and one little nose.
One little mouth and two little ears.
Two little eyes for smiles and tears.
One little head and two little feet.
One little chin which makes me complete!

One, Two, Buckle My Shoe

One, two, buckle my shoe.
Three, four, shut the door.
Five, six, pick up sticks.
Seven, eight, lay them straight.
Nine, ten, let's do it again!

Five Live Fish

One, two, three, four, five,
Catching fishes all alive.
Why did you let them go?
Because they bit my finger so.
Which finger did they bite?
The little finger on the right.

One for the Money

One for the money,
Two for the show,
Three to get ready,
And four to go!

Children's Literature: The following is a list of recommended children's books that may be used while teaching a unit on numbers.
- *Anno's Counting Book Big Book* by Mitsumasa Anno (HarperTrophy ©1992)
- *My First Number Book* by DK Publishing (DK Preschool ©2003)
- *The Icky Bug Counting Book* by Jerry Pallotta (Charlesbridge Publishing ©1992)
- *The Right Number of Elephants* by Jeff Sheppard (HarperTrophy ©1992)

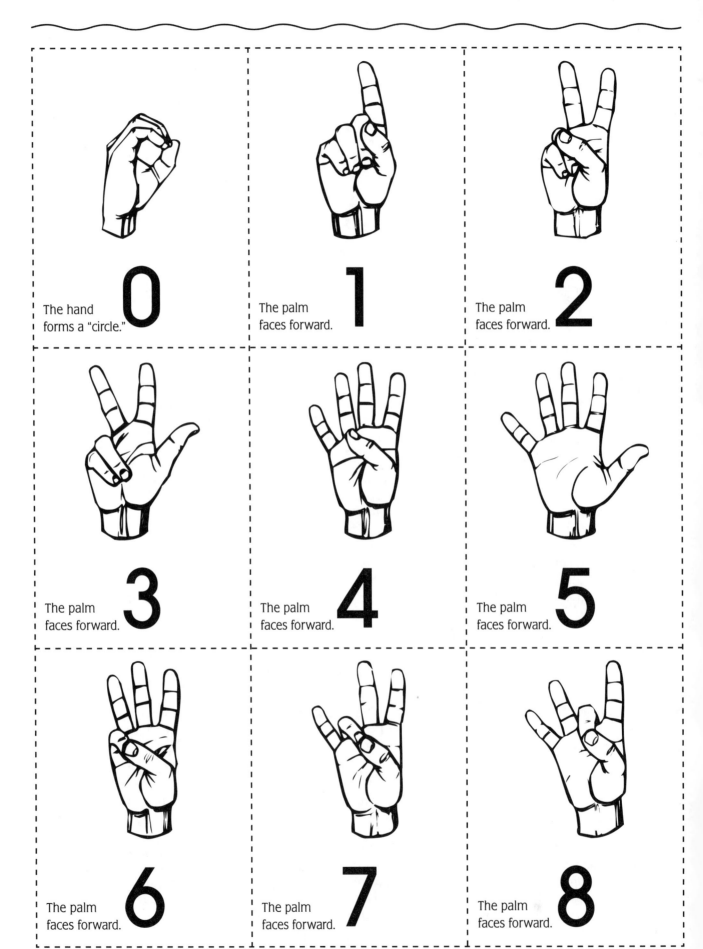

0
The hand forms a "circle."

1
The palm faces forward.

2
The palm faces forward.

3
The palm faces forward.

4
The palm faces forward.

5
The palm faces forward.

6
The palm faces forward.

7
The palm faces forward.

8
The palm faces forward.

9

The palm faces forward.

10

Extend the "A" hand shape and shake.

Flick the pointer finger up with the palm of the hand facing the body.

11

Flick the pointer and middle fingers up with the palm of the hand facing the body.

12

Make the sign for the number "3" and move the fingers up and down with the palm of the hand facing the body.

13

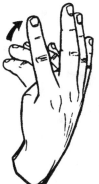

Make the sign for the number "4" and move the fingers up and down with the palm of the hand facing the body.

14

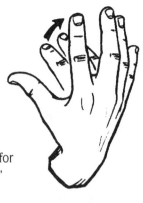

Make the sign for the number "5" and move the fingers up and down with the palm of the hand facing the body.

15

Sign "10" and then "6."

16

Sign "10" and then "7."

17

Sign "10" and then "8."

18

Sign "10" and then "9."

19

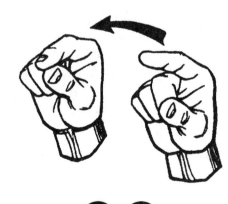

Pinch the pointer finger and thumb together

20

· Chapter Fifteen ·

Putting It All Together: Phrases

7 Individual Signs: like, see, what, when, where, who, why

11 Signed Phrases: Time to listen. Time to play. Time for a story. Line-up please. Please come here. I don't want . . . I don't know. I don't like . . . Do you want to play? Please sit down. See you later.

Make a copy for each child's "My Own Sign Language Dictionary," the Classroom Sign Word Wall, and one to be sent home to each child's parents.)

like
The thumb and pointer finger pinch together by the chest and move outward as if pulling the heart.

see
The open right hand makes the letter "V" with the palm facing toward the body. The fingers point toward the eyes and then pull away.

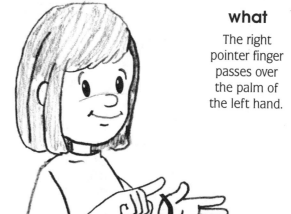

what
The right pointer finger passes over the palm of the left hand.

when
The left pointer finger is held straight up and the right pointer finger then makes a clockwise circle around the left finger.

where
The pointer finger is held up and shaken side to side.

who

The pointer finger makes a counterclockwise circle in front of the lips.

why

The fingertips of the right hand touch the forehead and then the hand moves out and changes to a letter "Y."

Time (to) listen.

time

The right pointer finger taps the left wrist several times on the spot where one would wear a watch.

listen

The hand is cupped behind the ear – implying that the ears should listen.

Time (to) play.

time

The right pointer finger taps the left wrist several times on the spot where one would wear a watch.

play

Both hands make the letter "Y" and twist back and forth at the same time.

Time (for a) story.

time
The right pointer finger taps the left wrist several times. on the spot where one would wear a watch.

story
The thumb and pointer fingers on both hands interlock, twist, and then pull apart which is the sign for "sentence." Do this several times to represent a story.

Line up please.

line up
Both hands make the letter "B" with the fingers apart and the left hand in front of the right. Then the fingers are pulled apart to represent a line of people.

please
The open hand is flat and moves in a circular motion on the chest.

Please come here.

please
The open hand is flat and moves in a circular motion on the chest.

come
Both pointer fingers beckon, or move, towards the body to indicate the concept of come.

here
Both hands are held palms up and make small circles in front of the chest.

I don't want _____.

I/me

Point to yourself using the pointer finger.

don't want

Make the sign "want" by placing both hands with fingers spread apart are brought in toward the body while the fingers curl up.

Then the hands are turned downward and outward as if to indicate that something is not wanted.

I don't know.

I/me

Point to yourself using the pointer finger.

don't know

Make the sign for "know" by touching the fingertips to the forehead, indicating that knowledge is in the brain.

Then the hand is moved away from the forehead showing a negative comparison.

I don't like _____.

I/me

Point to yourself using the pointer finger.

don't like

Make the sign for "like" by pinching the thumb and pointer finger together by the chest and then the hand is moved outward as if pulling the heart. Next move the hand outward with the fingers pointing away from the body.

(Do) you want (to) play?

play
Both hands make the letter "Y" and twist back and forth at the same time.

you
The pointer finger is pointed straight ahead.

want
Both hands, with fingers spread apart, are brought in toward the body while the fingers curl up.

Please sit down.

please
The open hand is flat and moves in a circular motion on the chest.

sit
The right pointer and middle fingers are draped over the same two fingers on the left hand. The fingers look like they are sitting.

See you later.

see
The open right hand makes the letter "V" with the palm facing toward the body. The fingers point toward the eyes and then pull away.

you
The pointer finger is pointed straight ahead.

later
The hand makes the letter "L" and moves forward from the side of the head in a downward movement.

        Sign Language Fun in the Early Childhood Classroom

Checklist of Signs

Name _____

Box 1 Date: ☐ ——————— Box 2 Date: ☐ ——————— Box 3 Date: ☐ ———————

Introduction:
☐☐☐— What's your name?
☐☐☐— My name is ___.
☐☐☐—Hello/Good-bye

Chapter 1: Manners and Everyday Words
☐☐☐—cleanup
☐☐☐—good
☐☐☐—listen
☐☐☐—no
☐☐☐—please
☐☐☐—share
☐☐☐—sing
☐☐☐—sorry
☐☐☐—thank-you
☐☐☐—toilet
☐☐☐—wash
☐☐☐—watch
☐☐☐—yes

Chapter 2: Following Directions
☐☐☐—come
☐☐☐—dance
☐☐☐—go
☐☐☐—jump
☐☐☐—roll
☐☐☐—run
☐☐☐—sit
☐☐☐—stand
☐☐☐—stop
☐☐☐—walk

Chapter 3: Emotions
☐☐☐—funny
☐☐☐—happy
☐☐☐—How do you feel?
☐☐☐—I love you.
☐☐☐—mad
☐☐☐—sad
☐☐☐—scared
☐☐☐—sick
☐☐☐—tired
☐☐☐—What's wrong?

Chapter 4: Colors
☐☐☐—color
☐☐☐—red
☐☐☐—blue
☐☐☐—yellow
☐☐☐—green
☐☐☐—orange
☐☐☐—purple
☐☐☐—brown
☐☐☐—black
☐☐☐—white
☐☐☐—pink

Chapter 5: Pets
☐☐☐—bird
☐☐☐—cat
☐☐☐—dog
☐☐☐—fish
☐☐☐—mouse
☐☐☐—pet
☐☐☐—rabbit

Chapter 6: Farm Animals
☐☐☐—animal
☐☐☐—chicken
☐☐☐—cow
☐☐☐—duck
☐☐☐—horse
☐☐☐—pig
☐☐☐—sheep

Chapter 7: Food/Eating
☐☐☐—apple
☐☐☐—banana
☐☐☐—cookie
☐☐☐—corn
☐☐☐—cracker
☐☐☐—drink
☐☐☐—eat
☐☐☐—hamburger
☐☐☐—hungry
☐☐☐—ice cream
☐☐☐—lunch
☐☐☐—milk
☐☐☐—more
☐☐☐—sandwich
☐☐☐—snack
☐☐☐—soup
☐☐☐—thirsty
☐☐☐—water

Chapter 8: People
☐☐☐—boy
☐☐☐—friend
☐☐☐—girl
☐☐☐—I/me
☐☐☐—man
☐☐☐—teacher
☐☐☐—woman
☐☐☐—you

Chapter 9: Family
☐☐☐—baby
☐☐☐—brother
☐☐☐—dad
☐☐☐—family
☐☐☐—grandma
☐☐☐—grandpa
☐☐☐—mom
☐☐☐—sister

Chapter 10: Weather
☐☐☐—cloud
☐☐☐—cold
☐☐☐—hot
☐☐☐—rain
☐☐☐—snow
☐☐☐—sun

Chapter 11: Toys
☐☐☐—ball
☐☐☐—block
☐☐☐—book
☐☐☐—game
☐☐☐—play
☐☐☐—puppet
☐☐☐—toy

Chapter 12: School Tools
☐☐☐—crayon
☐☐☐—glue
☐☐☐—paint
☐☐☐—pencil
☐☐☐—paper
☐☐☐—scissors

Chapter 13: Everyday Objects
☐☐☐—chair
☐☐☐—coat
☐☐☐—door
☐☐☐—flower
☐☐☐—hat
☐☐☐—shoes
☐☐☐—table
☐☐☐—window

Chapter 14:Numbers
☐☐☐—zero
☐☐☐—one
☐☐☐—two
☐☐☐—three
☐☐☐—four
☐☐☐—five
☐☐☐—six
☐☐☐—seven
☐☐☐—eight
☐☐☐—nine
☐☐☐—ten
☐☐☐—eleven
☐☐☐—twelve
☐☐☐—thirteen
☐☐☐—fourteen
☐☐☐—fifteen
☐☐☐—sixteen
☐☐☐—seventeen
☐☐☐—eighteen
☐☐☐—nineteen
☐☐☐—twenty

Chapter 15: Putting It All Together: Phrases
☐☐☐—like
☐☐☐—see
☐☐☐—what
☐☐☐—when
☐☐☐—where
☐☐☐—who
☐☐☐—why

☐☐☐—Time to listen.
☐☐☐—Time to play.
☐☐☐—Time for a story.
☐☐☐—Line-up please.
☐☐☐—Please come here.
☐☐☐—I don't want . . .
☐☐☐—I don't know.
☐☐☐—I don't like . . .
☐☐☐—Do you want to play?
☐☐☐—Please sit down.
☐☐☐—See you later.